D0338745

FOLLOWING THE PATH

FOLLOWING
THE PATH

The Search for a Life of Passion, Purpose, and Joy

JOAN CHITTISTER

I
IMAGE

New York

Copyright © 2012 by Joan D. Chittister

All rights reserved.
Published in the United States by Image, an imprint of the
Crown Publishing Group, a division of Random House, Inc.,
New York.

IMAGE is a registered trademark, and the "I" colophon is a
trademark of Random House, Inc.

Library of Congress Cataloging-in-Publication Data is available
upon request.

ISBN 978-0-307-95398-8
eISBN 978-0-307-95399-5

Printed in the United States of America

Jacket design by Nupoor Gordon
Jacket photograph: © William Huber/Getty Images
Author photograph: Ed Bernik

10   9   8   7   6   5   4   3   2   1

First Edition

Contents

Dedication and Acknowledgments

I knew years before it finally happened what I really wanted to do in life. In the meantime, I did lots of other things, all good but never quite "right," never quite satisfactory. Most people know that feeling, I'm sure. Most of us struggle for years to find our place in life. The question is, why is it such a difficult task to finally realize what we're meant to do and, if we're lucky, eventually discover the way to do it? This book looks at the kind of things that hold us back from becoming who we are and yet, at the same time, prod us unerringly toward it.

It unmasks the impact of other people's attitudes and values on our own. It considers the effect of both personal and public views on the choices we make in life, the works to which we give ourselves, the paths we pursue from one stage of development to another. It faces the fact that few life decisions are really made alone. In fact, they are often a by-product or a gift of the environment in which they emerge.

It is these things, as well as our own appetite for the future stirring within us, that influence who we are and what we become and why we can do what we do.

I know, for instance, that I might not be writing these lines right now if it had not been for a high school English teacher who figured me out long before I had even begun to figure myself out.

The great truth is that it is the people around us and what they think and see and believe about us that also bring us to the point where we can see and believe those things of ourselves. With their help we finally discover the connection between finding a job and making a life.

For many, the personal decisions that shape the way we live our lives come, far too often, as a result of what significant others in our lives think we should do. Parents, friends, and institutions expend a great deal of effort in the attempt to recruit our lives on behalf of their interests.

All I ever really wanted to do in life was to write. I wanted to think things out and then put those thoughts on paper. Like all the eminent writers whose works I had studied, I wanted to help the great conversations of life go on stirring the human soul to even deeper insights into human possibility.

What I didn't know was how to go about it. There simply was no niche, no professional outlet for a woman writer. There was also no place to simply sit down in the midst of life and do it.

So, I did small things on the side. I wrote small pieces after my real work was done. I managed a kind of professional contribution here and there. But, given the other demands of every day, nothing substantial.

Until.

Until two couples from two different parts of the world simply came out of nowhere in my life and offered the place, the natural environment, the time for reflection, and the concentration it takes to risk writing an English sentence for all the world to read.

Bill and Elizabeth Vorsheck and Gail and Sean Freyne have made a writer's life possible for me for over twenty years. I never solicited such a gift from either of them; they each simply offered it out of the generosity of their hearts and their own personal insights. The rest, as they say, is now commonplace, now real.

For that reason, I am doing more than simply inscribing a line of dedication in this book, *Following the Path*, to them. Their gift has, in fact, taken me far beyond the level of personal gratitude. Thanks to what I see in the importance of what they have done for me personally, I offer these comments as a clue to the significance of supporting others in their own search for passion, purpose, and joy.

What these families have done the world called "patronage" in centuries past. Thanks to patrons, to people who supported the work of others, art flourished, architecture bloomed, musical forms thrived, science prospered, and writing became the staple of civilization.

The conclusion is clear: the assistance we offer others as they attempt to find and follow the path that takes them to the best of themselves is key to the great adventure of life, our own perhaps, as well as theirs.

For these bearers of belief in my own life, for Bill and Betsy, for Gail and Sean, I am immensely grateful, immensely indebted.

And I am beholden for this particular work, in different ways, to others as well:

Without thinkers, both young and old, who also took their roles in the production of this work equally seriously—by prodding it into better shape, stretching it beyond its first self, assessing its insights—whatever finish, polish, and level of ideas that mark this final presentation might never have come to pass.

They are Kelly Adamson, Michele Canning, Kathy Felong, Gail Freyne, Christine Lundt, Rev. James Piszker, Sara Pitzer, Sisters Carolyn Gorny-Kopkowski, Mary Ellen Plumb, Marlene Bertke, Susan Doubet, Anne McCarthy, and Mary Lou Kownacki.

I am aware, too, of a real appreciation for my editors, John Burke and Gary Jansen, who were the fountainhead of this idea. Because of their willingness to be part of the good conversations on this topic, so many important ideas were spun.

Finally, I know that without my staff, who each

bring the best editing, thinking, dreaming, and challenging ideas they have to every page of every manuscript, without these people and the kind of dedication they give to this work, there would be no books at all.

I am especially aware of my dependence on S. Maureen Tobin, who makes it all happen around me; to Sisters Susan Doubet and Marlene Bertke, who check every word and put it all together, time after time after time; to S. Anne McCarthy, who reads with a critic's eye and a scholar's heart; and to S. Mary Lou Kownacki, whose conversations on the theme and whose readings of the work are invaluable to the both the poetry and the profundity of the final draft.

All these careful appraisers of its message are an integral part of this writing as surely as if it were their own.

Life is, indeed, a social experiment. What we do for one another we do together. My hope is that those who bring their own hearts and minds and lives to this finished work now will also come to the fullness of themselves so that the effects of that on our society will be infinitely good. For all our sakes.

In Palazzo Rezzonico, Venice,

By the Grand Canal, within

Sound of San Marco's clock tower

Lay Robert Browning, vigorously dying.

Someone brought him Asolando to hold,

His new book; and for a moment he

Riffled the pages; then he said

"I have given my life to that,"

And tossed it down lightly on the bed.

Finding the Way Home to Myself

It wasn't any kind of special moment when it happened. It wasn't my birthday, for instance, or an anniversary of anything. It wasn't even a family reunion or a great community event. I was just sitting somewhere, gazing into space, doing nothing whatsoever of significance or importance or even of any particular kind of enjoyment. I was just sitting, on an ordinary day in the midst of the ordinary things of life, waiting for a friend to arrive. And then it happened. The gentlest sense of wholeness and down-deep satisfaction came over me that I have ever known. It enfolded me like warm mist and calmed me to the core. Every ounce of taut energy so common to the demands of daily life in a technological society had been drained, it seemed. Only the feeling of being totally, quietly, completely alive remained. Then I realized what it was: I was happy. Happy. That's all. Just happy.

It felt within me like the stillness of an inland lake. I looked back over all the open meadows and tangled underbrush of my life and knew in an instant, like the snap of a shutter on a digital camera, that whatever had been, it had been right. Where I had been born was right, how I had lived life had been right, even all its wrong parts had been right.

But it has not always been thus. There were hollow, gaping times of uncertainty on the time line of my life when the direction seemed wrong or the path it promised was at best a dull and dreary dead end. Those were not happy times. They were times that were productive, even successful by some standards, perhaps, but not happy.

Later, still quietly touched by the experience, I read a line that made me pause. "Life," the philosopher Søren Kierkegaard wrote, "can only be understood backwards, but it must be lived forwards." At that moment, I decided to write this book. Clearly I had lived life forward long enough to understand how it is that we can get to feel such a moment of rightness, to know such satisfaction, to come to such happiness.

The pity is, I think, that there are so many others still "living it forward" who get very little help in doing so. So many young men stand ready to live leaping through life, so many young women now wait champing to take on its challenges, so many of the middle-aged stand at the ready for more of it, so many older people grow sad at its apparent going. All of them are full of high hopes and great aspirations, but unsure what to do with them and left with little time to try to think life through. They have hardly a moment in their fast-paced lives to do much more than get out of bed every day and try to make a living, try to pay the bills, try simply to keep up.

For many others, without the skills or the social supports it takes to have options in life, keeping up is beyond reach. For these people, existence itself seems to be life's one great project. The vision of "the good life," a real life, fullness of life, takes on the character of dim and distant fantasy.

In such a world as this, there is little room for dreaming about new designs for living, about over-arching purposes, about becoming the fullness of the self. Given these challenges, we can't plague ourselves with the great work of life; simply finding a job and settling down is enough to consume all our energies. Planning for a new tomorrow in the midst of an over-whelming present overwhelms the soul. Even trying to understand, in the course of getting by, what happiness might really be about can lead us to the edge of despair.

Instead, we struggle for years just to get established in something, just to accrue the basics—the educa-tion, the job, the independence—it takes to build the life we think we want. It doesn't take long to discover, however, that even when the basics of life get set-tled, little is really settled. Then there are only more obligations to meet, more people to report to, more events to attend, and so much more work to do that daring to think beyond the present moment becomes only another burden—an irritation, in fact.

Or, worse, when life seems, on the surface, to be stable but we cannot come to peace with a sense of being unfinished, we find ourselves thinking about nothing but the great questions of our lives, about the decisions that agitate within them. We ruminate forever about them. The questions never end: Should I go there? Or should I do this? Should I leave this? Should I try something else, do something entirely new? Should I go to this place or that, to this company or that, to this country or that, to this commitment or that? What am I really meant to do in life—and how will I know? What are the criteria for a happy life?

The trouble is that we seldom ever really get the time to struggle through the implications of such burdensome decisions slowly and carefully, calmly and methodically.

Few of us have the luxury of parsing possibilities and thinking them through with someone else who might expand our thinking or test our motives with us. We seldom have the freedom—economically or socially— simply to drift till something comes along that seems totally suited to who we think we know ourselves to be. So how can we know what we're meant to do with our lives? And how are we going to do it?

The default position is simply to go on from day to

day, tamping down the agitation, hoping to outgrow it. Until, one day, suddenly, we are confronted with a moment for making major life decisions we can no longer avoid. The now descends upon us urgently, bluntly. And by that time, it's too late for dissecting our doubts.

Something must be done—however spare the time we have had to consider the consequence of doing it—about life in the future as well as about life as it looks right now. There is no more time for deciding. A choice must be made or that one great chance to be happy may be lost forever, may never be possible again.

On what grounds can we possibly make it?

Most of us strike out in a given direction, magnetized by some minor aspect of it or simply grateful to have a starting place. We live in hope that this languid leap of faith will sweep us up into whatever it is that we have been born with the heart, the talent, the personality, the skills, and the commitment to do. The question is will it? And if it doesn't, then what? After all, I am making a life decision. For me, yes. But just as surely, for the sake of the rest of the world who need what I have to give and whose lives will be affected by mine—for better or for worse.

Everywhere there are stories of people with little who do small things in life and are supremely happy. They collect blankets for the homeless in winter, shop for the homebound, organize play activities for neighborhood children whose parents have to choose between providing companionship for their children and providing food for them. How do we explain that kind of happiness?

Everywhere there are stories of people who choose a path in life. And then, barely into it, discover that where they are is not where they should be if they are ever to become what they are meant to be. A story celebrating a small city's 73rd Annual Lion's Club Save an Eye football game in 2011, for instance, opens with the profile of a past player for whom the game had been a life-changing event, not once but twice. The story in the local newspaper reads:

"It was 1953 and at eighteen Bill Vorsheck thought he knew exactly what he wanted in life—a high school diploma, marriage to his neighborhood sweetheart and a job in a local plant. Several colleges offered the young football star scholarships, but he wasn't interested. He didn't realize, however, how much he would miss football after graduation and he soon learned that high school grads didn't get the area's dream jobs. Just two months after graduation, Bill faced what seemed like a long and dismal future.

"Then came the invitation to play in the 15th annual Erie Lion's Club Save an Eye Football Game. Bill knew it was a chance of a lifetime to play his beloved game one last time in this prestigious event in front of 10,000 local fans and he played his heart out.

"Vorsheck," the article goes on, "hauled down two straight passes in the fourth quarter for 19 yards and made 105 yards on the receiving end of five aerials. . . . Although the County lost as predicted, Bill was named the game's Most Valuable Player for his outstanding efforts.

"Exhilarated and ears still ringing from the thunder of the crowd, Bill entered the locker room after the game and found five college scouts awaiting his return with scholarship offers in hand. Life changed in a moment of team defeat but personal glory.

"One week later Bill was enrolled and playing ball for a [nearby] university on a full football scholarship. After graduating with his Bachelor of Science in Education, Bill held several teaching jobs in the area . . . where he was both teacher and [coach]. He eventually settled down as a social studies teacher and head football and track coach . . . By the 1960s life was steady and good for Bill and his young family."

Years later he told me, "After two months in that factory, I knew one thing for sure: I did not belong there." The winning young coach who had played his heart out, would now coach his heart out and lead his own team to victory in the 1967 Save an Eye game. As a result, this time he made friends with men whose mentoring would lead him to his final and fulfilling vocation of helping others develop themselves to the fullest but this time as a registered hypnotherapist.

He wasn't coaching sports anymore; he was coaching people beyond the defeats of their lives to success as human beings.

The story is not an unusual one. The path to the wholeness of the self commonly leads through a labyrinth of possibilities, a maze of gifts. The fact is that coming to fullness of life is seldom a straight line. It is a matter of learning to listen to the call—to the magnet of the heart within us—to assess our own gifts, to follow our own passions, and to find, through them, the happiness that flows from the fit between passion and purpose.

Happiness, I have come to understand, comes when what I choose to be about in life is actually worth spending my life doing. My life. This one life, with all its passions and with all its gifts. I remember the struggle to determine where happiness was for me as if I were still in the middle of that long-ago wrestling match with life. In fact, maybe I still am. Maybe we all are. Maybe nobody is ever really sure that what they have done was the absolutely right thing to do— at least not until life itself is very close to being over. Then and only then can we really ask ourselves if what we have done with our lives really made us happy. Was it really what our very being fitted us to do? Did it bring me to wholeness as a human being? Was it worth doing? And, if it is happiness I seek, what is happiness anyway? What are its criteria?

One thing for sure: happiness comes at a cost. It

requires that we make great long-range choices at the
very moment it most seems that short-term choices
will do. It means that we must discover who we are
and what we are called to do with our lives. It means
that we must determine both what the world needs
and what we have to give it. And having discovered
that, we must set our hearts to doing it, whatever the
obstacles, however long the way. Otherwise, what is
life about?

This book deals, then, with the fundamental question of "call," of finding direction and meaning in life,
of determining where we do—and do not—fit. To
discover what we're meant to do—what it is that will
really make us happy—and what we want to do with it
for the sake of the rest of the world is the very apex of
life. Deciding what we must do to be happy ourselves
so that we can be a gift to the world around us is the
central question of life. It is a question that deserves
serious reflection, that requires a long look at the self,
and that brings with it the rewards of a life well lived.

The question of how to lead a meaningful life is
the universal commonplace of humanity, the glue that
binds the world together. There is no age that has not
dealt with the questions of place and role in society,
no culture that has not attempted to define the meaning of meaning. But at the end of the day, it is ours
and ours alone to decide for ourselves. The question of
what each of us is meant to do in life is the question
that no one else can answer for us. It is the question of

uniqueness. It is the moral imperative of every human life. To discover and pursue what we are called to do in life is the very fundament of happiness.

The concept of call has, until our time with its new understanding of person, personal development, and psychological fulfillment, invariably been associated with religious ministries and special tasks. To withdraw from the average lifestyle of the average person in order to do God's own work in God's sacred places, the religions taught, was a divine imperative, a distinctive role in life, a special vocation. The rest of the people in society simply lived a good life in the best ways they knew how.

This ancient theology of vocation—the notion of having a special call from God that separated a person from the rest of the world—was well developed and long-standing. It was a matter of destiny, of knowing somewhere in the soul of us that we had been chosen.

A Jewish story describes the process well. When asked why he became a rabbi, the old man answered, "In the slaughter house, to determine the percentage of meat reserved for kosher, the executioner counts the cattle coming down the chute 1-2-3-4-5-6-7-8-9- and then says of every tenth kine, 'and one for God.' I knew that I was one of those."

From this perspective, a call was something that simply happened to someone, without explanation, without cause. Martin Luther called it "a stroke of fate." Some of us were "picked out" of the pack, some were not, and we knew who we were. To have a vocation meant having the mark of God on the soul of the one reserved to do the work of God. A person with a call to a religious life was to accept it and be content.

For others the call was a command from God to sacrifice our lives for the sake of the glory of God. Whether we wanted to or not. Whatever else we were unable to do as a result of it.

A vocation, from these perspectives, was an end in itself, not a unique gift particular to the person or even a particularly intense or magnetizing interest in any particular aspect of ministry. It meant simply giving one's life over to be disposed of in the service of religion and of God, as life saw fit.

But at the same time, those same two qualities—knowing that we have within us something that marks each of us in a special way and that this quality has been given to us for some reason greater than ourselves—are the essence of coming to wholeness. The task of determining what that quality is and what to do with it is the single great work of being alive.

In our time, then, another shift in the understanding of what it means to have a vocation, to be called to something particular in life, is in process. In this age, the uniqueness of the individual and Paul's teaching to the Corinthians that multiple gifts are given by God for the sake of the community has brought us to a new point. We take Paul seriously now. We are all called, we know now, to do our part in the ongoing creation of the world. In this age, both theology and psychology concur on the uniqueness of the individual and the notion that different individuals have different gifts for the sake of the upbuilding of the whole human enterprise.

It is at this new point in history that choice becomes both a blessing and a bane. Life is no longer a matter of either accepting destiny or simply following patterns set for us by generations long past. It is now the basis of the spiritual quest, the wholeness of the soul. Now we take ourselves seriously, as well.

We are, we know now, each called to something special, simply by virtue of being alive, simply by being endowed with these particular gifts, simply by being left with an unfinished world, surely by being a co-creator of the universe. "Till the garden and keep it," the Judaeo-Christian scriptures teach us in the creation story. Clearly, we are each responsible for living our individual gifts full heartedly. Out of the depth of our souls. Out of a sense of moral responsibility. "I put before you death and life," those same scriptures say. "Choose life!" That is our call.

A call, we have come to understand, commits us. Each of us. All of us. Individually. We come to realize that whatever gifts we may each have, however difficult it is for me to give myself to it, the giving of it is exactly what I have been born to do. When those two things—when individual gifts and the human thirst for them—come together for me, that is my call. Not my job. My call.

When my life takes that shape, when I know that I have lived my life out of that gift and that commitment, then, at that moment, happiness overcomes me and I know that I have come home to myself.

This book is about what it takes to find and respond to the magnet within us—that great, deep passion for life toward which our hearts leap up at every turn. This is the call that demands that we give back to life everything that life has given to us. Then, at some moment far from now, perhaps, the feeling will finally come that, looking back, whatever difficulties we have suffered in its doing, it has all been right.

This book is meant to give someone in the process of making a life decision at any age—in early adulthood, at the point of middle-age change and later, when we find ourselves at the crossroads without a name—some ideas against which to pit their own minds, their own circumstances. Its purpose, as they wrestle with the process of trying to find and follow their own special call at this new stage of life, is to both provoke thinking and to clarify it.

I decided to write this book because I am at the stage of life myself now where being able to look backward is an important credential, too much underrated and too often overlooked. But it is precisely the perspective of time and experience that may help the next set of beginners to go forward, to uncover all the aspects of the question of meaning in life before agreeing to become anything other than themselves.

Hopefully those who in middle age find themselves in reach of another moment in their long-lost search for fulfillment can take courage from realizing that even a person's sense of meaning in life can happen in stages.

And finally it may help those, too—for whom most great public decision making is now largely over—to come to understand their own lives, to complete them, if necessary, and to make peace with the circuitousness of its journey to fulfillment. Then that warm mist of happiness which the philosopher Aristotle said could not possibly come much before the end of life can finally be quietly, serenely wallowed in.

Life is a pure flame, and we live by an invisible sun within us.

THOMAS BROWNE

1.

THE SEARCH FOR HAPPINESS
AND MEANING IN LIFE

*"If you never liked being an accountant,
why did you stay in it for thirty years?" I
asked him.*

*"Well, it was steady and the money was
good," he said.*

We use a raft of words for happiness in this world: delight, enjoyment, contentment, fun, excitement, pleasure, cheerfulness. But none of them really hits the mark. At most they describe feelings that come and go with the wind. They all describe something that exists in relationship to something else. When the party is over, the delight goes with it. When the Ferris wheel stops, the excitement ends, too.

No, happiness cannot possibly be any of those fleeting, transitory things. Happiness is a great deal more than any impulse and its dependence on the mood of the moment. Happiness exists on its own. It is a steady-state operation of the soul. It sees every day through a filter of basic satisfaction.

Traditional definitions of a person's call in life, however, never mentioned happiness as one of its dimensions. At least not happiness here, on earth, while I live. Thomas Aquinas, the great philosopher-theologian of the thirteenth century, for instance, argued that happiness had to do with union with God. Happiness was earned during our lifetime but was not necessarily expected to be enjoyed here on earth. Happiness, real happiness, this theology implied, could only really be expected when death united us with God. Earthly happiness was not a topic in this catechism.

A call in life, in that world, meant to give one's life to God, in some particular religious way. And even then there was no notion that a person would necessarily see it as a way to fulfill the search for personal happiness on earth. It meant simply to do the will of God, however difficult.

Those called to religious ministry should simply accept the duty as inevitable, as much the will of God as it was of any other dimension of personal choice. What accounted for that destiny, however, what it was that explained how that destiny got forged—other than the oblique or whimsical will of God, of course— who knew? Most of all, how a person might recognize the will of God in their regard or what might make that sacrifice possible, let alone a happy choice, went unexamined.

In these theologies of life, the fact that a call to ministry was defined as a call from God sufficed. There was nothing else to know about the justification for choosing it, nothing else to desire, nothing else against which to gauge the value of it. Merely to have thought of it was sign enough of its reality.

In each case, simply doing something good, something institutionally religious, apparently, was enough. Human happiness was not the issue. The notion that being happy with something might be one of the signs of having a call to it was entirely beneath consideration.

Except we know now that it's not. Happiness, we have come to understand, is the driving force of life. It is the Holy Grail of human development. It gives to whatever we decide to do its dynamism. Happiness is the torch of life, the fire within, the very galvanism of our existence. And science, of all things, confirms that.

Neurologists have discovered that the brain is configured for happiness. We were born to be happy, just as much as we were born to communicate or to love or to reason. The very physiology of the brain is designed for happiness—which is why mood-changing drugs work. They satisfy the needs of our neurological chemistry and lift us out of depression or calm us into serenity.

Not to be happy, therefore, to be regularly dispirited or sad or negative, is not only not normal but it is also an indicator of either life or chemistry gone wrong. Whole institutions and occupations have sprung up to help people find happiness. Their findings rank among the most startling scientific discoveries of the twenty-first century.

Medicine, too, has for years warned about the relationship between stress and physical sicknesses. To live in long-term situations that wear us down, wear us out, sour our hearts, and choke our hopes will soon show up in our bodies, they tell us. And yet we know that some people live in very difficult circumstances, even seek them out as doctors in African villages, for instance, as caregivers in hospices, as counselors in detention facilities, as total-care providers for crippled children and spouses and never seem to wear down. What's the difference between choosing lives like that and being stressed to the breaking point by them? And what does that have to do with finding meaning, with having a call to a particular commitment, a special place in the world?

Psychologists, as well, recognize now that there is a set point for happiness in the human being that affects the way we see the world. This underlying perspective and attitude toward life in each of us is fundamental but not determinative. Just as there is a set point for blood pressure and weight gain and body temperature in each of us that can be affected even if it cannot be permanently changed, there is a stable range of positive emotional responses in us, too, that can be shaped and reshaped in life. We can meliorate difficult situations and make life happy again. We can make changes. We can discover where we need to go to be happy and then take steps to get there. We can learn to distinguish the kinds of stress that invigorate us from the kinds of stress that deplete us and make the choices that give us life.

I have known, for instance, what it is like to be sick but happy at the same time. I've lived with the effects of polio all my adult life and never, ever counted that among the things that made me unhappy. Tired, yes; limited in some ways, maybe, but not unhappy. And I have also known what it is to be doing something good, like teaching rather than writing, and be unhappy at the same time.

It's not difficult to understand that happiness is real. We have felt its fleeting presence. We know the depth of the pit within us waiting to be filled with it. We have seen happiness in people whose lives we doubt we ourselves could ever possibly bear: in paraplegics, of all people; in the poor who have nowhere near the things we have to ease our way through life; in the forgotten ones from nameless barrios who come into our plush living rooms on TV screens.

No, it's not the possibility of happiness we doubt. It is how to find it that eludes us. The real challenge of life, then, is to understand what happiness is so that, from beginning to end, we steer our lives in that direction. If we feel a strong call to do something in life and never do it, can we possibly be happy? If we don't really know what happiness is and follow the wrong star in the wrong direction, are we doomed? In that case can we ever find happiness at all?

It all depends.

One thing for sure, in our world happiness has become big business. We sell it in cosmetic bottles and buy it in weight loss programs. We're told that it's in marriage and then later that it's in divorce. We expect it from our families and, when that fails, hope that by starting over again with total strangers—in another company and another city and another position with more pay—that we'll do better the next time.

And why doesn't it happen if, as the scientists say and our hearts insist, we're all really meant to find it? Because as the Greek philosophers knew centuries ago, happiness doesn't come from the outside of us. Happiness comes from the inside. Happiness has something to do with what we do with who we are. Clearly, pleasure and happiness are not synonyms.

That's why the momentary euphoria of drugs and alcohol only makes us miserable in the end. That's why power and money only leave us in dismay at the end. That's why one more house and two more cars and the big new boat leave us engorged with things and empty, empty of heart.

Aristotle, the great philosopher of personal development, said happiness depended on developing ourselves to our fullest potential. On becoming the best self we can possibly be. On doing what we do for the sake of a better world. He didn't call happiness a virtue. He said happiness depended on our commitment and involvement in "virtuous activity." In doing good.

It is easy for those with resources to do a lot of things. We can travel, for instance, and sample every food of every culture. We can find thrills in theme parks and casinos, in racetracks and rock concerts. We can spend years acquiring money and things, renovating property and selling it at a profit, climbing ladders—anybody's ladders, in either church or state—and at the end, when it is all over, when there are no more summits to climb, no more prizes to win, we find ourselves still restless, still unfulfilled, more fearful of loss than we are satisfied by what we have gained. Then we understand the power of Aristotle's definition of happiness. It is not *activity*, Aristotle says, that happiness is about; it is *virtuous* activity on which he grounds the search for it. It's about doing something that makes the world a better place to be.

What fills the heart with happiness, ironically enough, is not what we get out of the world; it's what we put into it. Being about something worthwhile, spending our lives on something worth spending a life on is what, in the end, makes us happy.

A creative God didn't complete creation, I am convinced, so that we might have the happiness that comes with continuing to co-create it ourselves.

If we really want to be happy, we need to find out

what we do best and do it to the utmost so that having done our part in this co-creation we can have the satisfaction such a life deserves. We need to learn that giving ourselves to something worth doing is more important, more valuable than giving ourselves only until something better, something more exciting, something more lucrative comes along.

The Sufi say, "For the raindrop, joy is entering the river." We need, like raindrops in the river, to learn to lose ourselves in what we were made to be. We need to find ourselves about something more in life than the social status and streams of glitter that we have allowed to define us.

Being happy is not something that just happens to anyone. It happens to those who discover who they are and what it is that's at the core of them—singing or cooking or planning or calculating. These people come to understand what it is in them that makes them unique. They discover what they really like to do in life, not simply what they do because everyone else does it. They determine what it is, of everything they do, that they do best. And then they choose what they can do with it for the good of the rest of the world.

This umbilical cord to the rest of the world is something we decide on consciously and clearly and then with great clarity of soul give ourselves to doing. I see happiness on the faces of wealthy people who serve soup in the local soup kitchen. I see it on the faces of young people who spend their summers building houses for people in mountain towns where coal mines closed and left generations of poorly educated people to fend for themselves. I see it in those who, after years of doing what everyone else wanted them to do, suddenly got up and started over somewhere else by developing their own gifts and becoming that gift to others.

But no one I know thinks it all happens in a straight line. No, life is far more exciting than that. It's learning to live it that matters. Finding our own particular challenge may be difficult at first. But we do. Finally. Eventually. However difficult the way.

Life is a foreign language; Everyone mispronounces it.

CHRISTOPHER MORLEY

2.

WHAT DOES ENJOYMENT HAVE TO DO WITH HAPPINESS?

"Take those earphones off your head and do something worthwhile."

"I am doing something worthwhile; I'm listening to music."

I learned very early in life that we all get two choices about how to live it: we can spend life amusing ourselves or we can take what engages us and turn it into a life. We can, as we've learned to say, spend our lives dabbling in a bevy of hobbies or we can embrace what energizes us and turn our hobbies—the things we love to do—into our lives.

We need to explore within us the distinction between enjoyment and happiness, between what amuses us and what expands us, between what gives us pleasure and what gives us satisfaction, the sense of an aim well met, a life well lived. It's not about economics; it's about attitudes. It's not about a job; it's about a passion. It's not about class; it's about will. For some of us, it's art lessons that lead us to become the local landscape artist. For others it's about a basketball hoop on a telephone pole on a city street that leads us years later to organize the local neighborhood teams.

There's a difference between knowing what I enjoy and knowing what makes me happy. Enjoyment is what I pursue in order to give life a spice and freshness that dailiness so often dulls. To play a game of chess against the computer once a day is enjoyment; to play chess in the same place, at the same time every day of my life would become achingly routine—and quickly. Enjoyment is about finding something that interrupts the sameness of life and at the same time sends me back to it refreshed and ready to begin again with new energy and a new sense of commitment. It's a few hours of music at the end of the day, maybe. Or karaoke on Friday nights. Or a basketball game on the weekend. Whatever the activity, it's a moment of release from responsibility that breaks through life's preoccupations and deletes, at least for a while, the unending stream of concerns that come with them.

I love to sit down at a keyboard every once in a while just to turn my mind away from ideas and let it drift into feeling. I've been known to walk away from the desk in the middle of the day to train my little parrot. Nothing washes away the drumbeat of the day for me nearly as completely as sitting on a pier with a fishing line in my hand. I have a friend, on the other hand, who reads a poem a day to free the mind from old ideas and surprise it with new ways of seeing things. Things like that—those freewheeling moments of pure delight, required by no one and needing no justification—free us from the tedium of the day and the tension that builds up inside us as the workload increases despite our ever more intense attempts to control it.

This ability to enjoy life is a rich and vital gift. It enables a person to bear stress well. It saves us from turning into robots, into slaves to either work or worry. It helps us to move from situation to situation, from one side of the country to the other and find a home there with strangers who enjoy what we enjoy. It enables us to make friends and to come down off the Mount Olympus of business or workaholism and develop our humanity as well as our skills.

The important thing to understand is that when we are doing what we really love doing, we are making the world around us a happier place for everyone. For others as well as for ourselves. When we're relaxed and refreshed, we ourselves become more pleasant for others to be around. As a result, our own happiness is a piece of happiness for them, as well as for ourselves. Happiness, then, is its own kind of sacred canon.

Most of all, perhaps, the things we enjoy go with us long after the work years are over. They can lead us into other whole dimensions of life. They can take us into nature in new ways. They can introduce us to people we would otherwise never have met in our own neighborhood or workplace or social circle. They can provide a kind of adventure to life far beyond what either work or home life contains. Enjoyment is the antidote to the abiding pace and patterns of life that dampen the spirit and mechanize our souls. No doubt about it: enjoyment is a perennial of happiness. But don't be fooled: enjoyment and happiness are not synonyms. Enjoyment is, at best, an answer to the rigors of routine; it is not the abiding sense of a life well lived. That comes with having lived life well at every level and to the very heart of its ultimate meaning.

What makes for happiness is something far beyond the tension-relieving quality of life's temporary distractions and even more than the quality of its passing interests. This sense of human fullness, whatever it is for each of us, is more than casual relief from the routines of life. Whatever form it takes, there is in happiness the kind of constant which enjoyment cannot bring us: happiness does not lie in filling time with delight; it is what makes my one life worthwhile. It sings a song of significance in the center of my soul. What makes me happy when I look back on my life as years go by is that I have done something with it that had meaning. I have done something that was larger than myself, that had meaning for someone else.

It is that kind of happiness that brings me to the fullness of myself.

What makes me happy is what directs my life. It is

the love of the land that keeps a farmer in the fields from dawn to dark. It is the desire to make life easier for others that keeps a woman who trains service dogs washing down kennels and sweeping up dog food every day of her life. It is the hours of research and months of fruitless experimentation that keep an oncologist up nights searching for a cure for the cancer patient she does not know. It is a concern for children that keeps an old woman caring for the babies of the neighborhood while their mothers work.

The qualities that flow from that kind of self-giving touch every layer of life that breathes in me: It consumes my energy. It gives me a sense of deep-down purpose in life. And in the end, it brings me a feeling of satisfaction and contentment, however difficult the doing of it. What makes us happy is whatever it is that causes us to lose ourselves and all our self-centeredness and all our pettiness and gain a heart as large as the world in the very process of doing it.

There are, the positive psychologists tell us, clear signs of happiness. When we're happy, the studies show, we lose a sense of time altogether. When we are doing what makes us happy, we do not watch clocks or tap our fingers till the period is over. In fact, we are likely to forget entirely what's next on the schedule, so absorbed are we in what we're doing now—this writing, this cooking, this program planning. When we're doing what makes us happy, anything other than that is easily ignored. No amount of schedules or notes or reminders or calls can dislodge us from the power of the moment we're in. This is often enjoyable, yes, but it is also more than simply enjoyment. It is the challenge of the intractable problem, the determined frustration that surrenders to persistence, the anticipation of the good that comes with the completion of my part of the task. With or without the words to say it, I know with every breath in me that this is what my life is supposed to be about.

I had an artist friend, a monk and potter, whose work has been collected by galleries and museums around the world—the Vatican Museum, the Smithsonian, the Tate—who told me once, "I started life believing that I was a monk who was also a potter and then realized that I was a potter who was also a monk." It was an admission of identity that shook me to the core. How many of us really know who we are? How many of us have really allowed ourselves to become the call to the self that is in us?

The difference between the joy of listening to music and the determination to use music to teach crippled children a life skill is the difference between doing what I like with my life and doing what I can do that the world really needs from me. Listening to music is enjoyment; using music to change the world is what Aristotle called "virtuous activity." Listening to music is for my enjoyment; enabling crippled children to develop the music within themselves improves life for others. The distinction between the two makes all the difference in the world. Literally. And all the difference in my own sense of complete contentment as the years go by.

At the same time, knowing what it is that we enjoy can be a clue to what has the capacity to make us really happy in life and life really happy with us. The two things are not unrelated. The music I loved as a child may well be what moves me to go into audio work as an adult. The physical therapist who taught me to walk again may fan the flame of the medical technician in me. The love of stories may tease the writer in me years later. Indeed, enjoyment may be the seed of the future, but happiness transcends the whims of enjoyment. Happiness is not made of moments; happiness is the harvest time of the soul.

The song of life is born in every soul. But the song we are meant to sing does not come to us whole. It grows in us—louder, stronger, clearer, more fully—over the years until we discover, finally, that our call has been within us all the while. Learning to hear the song within us, finding the call within us, and then bending our lives to follow it to the fullness of ourselves is the key to happiness, to meaning, to fullness of life.

A bird does not sing because it has an answer.
It sings because it has a song.
CHINESE PROVERB

3

WHAT DOES IT MEAN TO BECOME THE FULLNESS OF OURSELVES?

"You're a very good welder," the wife said. "Why don't you start your own business?"

"Not on your life," the husband said. "It's too much of a risk."

"Family," I know now—having seen how other people go about it—was more an ideal to me than a reality. Where I came from, family was about bloodlines, not relationships. My mother, the youngest of thirteen, hardly knew her older brothers and sisters. Each of them, she said, had dispersed across the country at an early age. A few had simply disappeared; one was killed in the war. "Most of them were gone before I was old enough to know them," she told me when I began to ask questions about who we were and where we'd come from.

I, on the other hand, was an only child in a nuclear family that was far distant for most of my growing-up years from any of the rest of it—uncles, aunts, grand-parents, and cousins. As a result, perhaps, family fas-cinated me, more perhaps than if I had lived in the center of them. As I began to travel, I began to look them up, if for no other reason than to see what we looked like as a clan, to find out who they were in real life rather than in my mother's old photograph album. To see, probably, how I myself was like them and how I was not. As a result, my memories of them are sparse but sharp.

In one instance I managed to visit an old aunt well into her eighties whom I had seen very few times in life and by that time, well over twenty years before this. She was living alone in a strip mall of small apart-ments by then, a clean and well-kept place but plain and simple. I was not prepared for what I found inside. The little three-room apartment was tightly furnished with the leavings of a life that had clearly known bet-ter times. But hung two deep on every wall, in heavy gilded, hand-carved frames, were oil paintings of con-siderable size. They were bright and strong and vibrant.

"Aunt Florence," I said with no small amount of amazement, "where did you get all these oil paint-ings?" The answer was at least as amazing as the work: "Why, I painted them myself," she said, her eyebrows arched, her voice firm. "I've always wanted to paint, so I took a course last year."

At a moment like that the life lessons about the

nature of happiness and its relationship to becoming the fullness of the self are almost too many to absorb at once. Clearly, what we are meant to do in life never really stops biting at our heels. Our unfinished selves never stop calling to us.

People start to search out what they're most interested in as children, as teenagers, as young adults. It may take years for the heart to find the soul of itself, to know what that really is, but it will happen. Someday. What we are really meant to do in life never ever stops shadowing our steps, pursuing us, plaguing our souls. People begin to paint when they are eighty and then live with a strange admixture of the joy of doing it and a tinge of regret, perhaps, for the way life could have been if only they had started earlier. If only.

We are what we are, but the gift of self unfolds only as we go, often barely noticeable, always with surprise. It can take years before it becomes clear—the real gift that is hidden within us. Which is why, perhaps, so few people end up in the professional fields they were prepared for as children and students but, if truth were known, never really wanted in the deepest parts of the heart of them.

Developing the honesty it takes to unmask the self to the self is no small task. Until we are able to uncover the real reasons we are doing what we're doing, there is no being sure if we are living into a call or living out a public expectation. In the process of coming to understand what it takes to come to the fullest development of the self, it is imperative to distinguish between what I am doing and why I want to do it. Without that, there is no hope for the liberation of the self, let alone the fulfillment of the self.

In the course of trying to respond to what I think may be my call to fullness of life, then, the fundamental task must be the identification of the driving forces in my own particular life. It's important to unmask why I chose one area over another as the place to begin my adult life. It may be simply because there was no other way into an area that interested me. So I took a job as a research assistant at a magazine in the hope that someday one of the editors would let me do a story of my own. Or maybe I took my first major job just simply to make the money I needed to do something else. That's ambition. That's healthy.

But if I did what I did—studied medicine, went to the seminary, worked in the family business—because someone else wanted me to do it, despite the fact that I wanted nothing to do with any of it, that's not personal ambition; that's puppetry. And the willingness to be a clone of someone else's ambitions will surely wear thin someday. Or just as bad, I may have done something precisely because someone else did not want me to do it. I may have chosen out of desperation. Or out of a need for approval. Or out of a desire to rebel. Or because I was looking for money rather than for happiness.

The more honest I am in examining my own motives for doing anything in life, the closer I am to being myself. The more equipped I am to distinguish the me I want to be from the me everybody else wants me to be, the more likely I am to become it.

If, in the middle of my life, then, I find myself on the verge of making a great change in life direction, the question is more important than ever. To know what it is that is bringing me to this point now can make the difference between real happiness and real pain. To find myself suffering from years of delayed ambitions is the sign to reassess whether what I have is worth giving up what I think I want. Boredom with the present situation may be a call to recognize a life not lived. A need to get away from the present situation may be a bad case of delayed adolescence or a cry to finally grow up and go on.

Or even later, at another stage of life, if my professional years have, for all practical purposes, come to an end, what is stopping me now from developing the parts in me that lie untested and untried—except perhaps the bogus notion that life ends with commercial retirement. As if an arbitrary number—meant to get one generation out of the workforce so that another one can enter it—is also an end to creativity and competence in another field.

Where does personal authenticity lie if not in moving inward to identify the obstructions I myself put between me and the call? When I refuse to listen to the dreams that cry within me for fullness of life, I fossilize myself. When I give way to the obstacles I create for myself, I doom myself to underdevelopment. Refusing to take for granted that barriers of money, opportunity, background, and professional preparation make another phase of life impossible opens the way to something new, even if not to everything at once.

But without authenticity about why I do what I do, how can I ever begin to do anything else, how can I ever be completely myself? To make a truly life-giving decision I need to have squarely faced what it is that gives me life. I need to find friends, professionals, spiritual directors who will help me—allow me—to speak my heart's cry aloud. I need to speak the truth of my interests, my abilities, my desires, my boredom, my dissatisfaction—even my long-time need to satisfy other people's plans for me. I need the help that comes from having my confusion and despair, my disappointment and angst accepted and understood by those who are not themselves threatened by what I might do with my own life. I need the acceptance and encouragement of others so that I can move on beyond fear, beyond stuckness, to the freedom of soul it takes to be the me I am.

I talked to a well-known massage therapist a while ago who specializes in orthopedic rehabilitation. She never started that work until she was fifty years old. She had known for years that she had a natural gift for body work, she said, but women did not do those things then.

By the time women were moving into the field, she was too old to begin that kind of study, she told herself. It was impossible to find courses such as that, her friends told her. It was a foolish kind of change for a woman who had been a teacher for years, the family said. But she began the course regardless. By the end of her very first day of courses she knew she had finally found what she really wanted to be. She had discovered what she did best. She knew, she said, what she had been born to do. And she did it.

There is a *me* in me, I understood when I heard her story—whoever we are, whatever we are now doing—that has been too long ignored, too soon repressed, and waiting to be discovered.

The power that comes with self-discovery at any age catalyzes us. It drives the young; it surprises the middle-aged; it emboldens those who might be tempted to declare life over before it has even truly begun. Now, I can stop doing what everyone else wants me to do and begin to care more about what God has fitted me to do.

It is enlightenment that life is really all about. Otherwise, we may go through the motions, look eminently successful, totally fulfilled, completely happy to others, but know inside ourselves that we failed in the end to have ever truly lived.

Knowing others is wisdom.
Knowing oneself is enlightenment.

LAO TZU

4.

WHOSE CALL IS IT?

"Where did you ever get such a ridiculous idea?"

"I don't know where it came from. I only know that I can't stop wanting to do it."

Life is a confusion of possibilities clear only to those who follow the drummer within. But who isn't aware how much more difficult that is than it sounds? In the first place, just knowing what we really do want to do—and why—is the arduous part of the process. Or as an Irish psychologist taught a group of psychotherapists in training, "Remember, lads, it isn't digging holes that's difficult for most people. It's figuring out where to dig them that's the problem."

The Irishism translates easily from culture to culture. Most of us don't resist the notion that we all have a work to do in life. We're just not sure what work that is or how to discover which of multiple interests is the one we should be pursuing. When people walk in the door looking for help, the Irish counselor wanted new therapists to know, they aren't there because they're afraid to make a decision. They're there because, in the face of competing goods in their lives, they don't know how to go about it. That's us he was talking about. And it's true.

In an age of mobility, the choices are vast, it seems; nothing is unthinkable. Or impossible, for that matter. Young people bicycle around the world these days, earning their keep as they go. The "Lost Boys" found themselves in the United States—a world away from the Sudan, where they had wandered orphaned and uncared for just a few years before. They were soon in school and on their way to becoming Americans.

Clearly, change and options are the order of the day. And yet, in the end, it is the self that prevails. A young cousin just out of a very average college took off for Asia to find his fortune in finance there. He returned to the States, of course, and settled down in a far more prosaic position, but he had followed his heart and discovered later that it was exactly where he had left it in the first place. At home surrounded by family. Sufficiency had taken the place of affluence in his young life; ambition had given way to happiness.

A young woman friend took a year off after medical school to work in a small clinic in Africa before going on to choose her specialization. What she found there gave her a sense of purpose far beyond the boundaries of mere professionalism. She discovered there that what her skills fitted her for was exactly what a world of dying children needed—pediatricians who specialize in infectious diseases. The trip to Africa both deepened her life and gave it direction.

An unmarried woman friend, after years in a successful career, adopted a foreign child who would certainly be either dead or grossly debilitated without her. This new and meaningful role as parent has become the centerpiece, the light, her whole reason to be alive. Reaching out to the other gave this single, successful, financially secure woman a whole new reason to be alive.

The stories are legion and the lessons in them bear serious consideration: what is there that can possibly stop us, not only from doing what we want to do but also from discovering what we're meant to do? Us, that's what. It's what we harbor within us that really determines what happens to us in life. It's self-knowledge that gives us direction in life. It's the values we bring to our decision-making that will determine both the integrity and the impact of our lives.

The truth is that, like a camera with a split-screen focusing system, we spend life trying to bring the two parts of us together—the public self and the private self—into one integrated whole. The private self, psychiatric theory calls "the self: the essence of humanity with which we're born." The public self, the part of us that is formed by our interaction with others, psychiatric theory calls the ego. It is the ego that has learned to conform to the expectations and attitudes society demands of us. What other people require of us leads us to create the masks we present to the world. For the sake of conforming or responding to the notions of others—parents, role models, mentors—we become docile, compliant, and, sometimes, trapped.

The private self wants to become the fullness of what it means to be fully human—to be what we are born to be, and have been given the gifts to be, and which, down deep, we have the raw and searing desire to be.

The public self wants to be approved, to be liked, to be successful, to be accepted—to be what society says we should be if we want to be accepted by it. In order to function well in it, we learn from infancy to respond to its very subtle but very clear signals. "Do this but do not do this" leads to "Yes, sir; Yes, sir; Yes, ma'am; Yes, ma'am." And it is those things, those internal struggles between who we are and who society expects us to be, that make doing what we know we are called to do so complex, so critical. It is the struggle between the self and the ego that binds us.

The Dweck study of differences between bright girls and average boys indicates that young girls hear themselves constantly defined as "very smart," or "very hardworking," or "very good" to the point that they believe that those traits are inborn and unchangeable. Boys, on the other hand, Dweck reports, are more likely to hear things like "If you just worked harder you could do this." As a result, the study concludes, girls grow to be women who think their place in life is fixed. Some things, they know because they have been told so, they do well; other things they don't. So, if they have difficulty doing something, they are more inclined to give up on it as impossible for them. Boys, on the other hand, learn to see difficulty as a challenge and work twice as hard at it. As life goes by, this kind of labeling can make all the difference in a person's ability to make choices, to attempt change, to try new things. It can obstruct personal growth, even in the brightest of us.

It is this very image-making process that clouds every life decision we face. To live up to public expectations, to get social approval, I take on the public norms. I become the perfect student at whatever cost to my social life. I become the willing worker, never mind overtime pay. I become the macho man and the female female—despite the fact that in the deepest part of the soul of me, I feel neither tough nor seductive.

I remember, for instance, being perfectly settled about my decision to enter a monastery—intent on it, in fact—until I saw the looks on people's faces. Some people responded with disbelief and disapproval. Some reacted with disdain. I could feel quiet reluctance even from people I was certain would value the idea—and me—for doing it. Then, as Shakespeare puts it, I had "to screw my courage to the sticking point" and wrestle

again with the very thought of it. What was the turning point? I told myself that if I did not go to the monastery as I planned, I would regret forever my failure to
at least try what I felt was my genuine call in life.

It is this step into the true self that makes all the
difference.

Following the call of the heart is not a guarantee that
we will make choices without consequences, decisions
without doubt. Life is not a carnival where fantasy is
reality and mistakes are benign. Life is an experience
of continual growth, of deepening insight. What was
right for me at one point of life may not be right at
all at another point. "Suddenly many movements are
going on within me, many things are happening," Me-
ridel Le Sueur wrote. "There is an almost unbearable
sense of sprouting, of bursting encasements, of moving
kernels, expanding flesh." And there is also an equally
burdensome sense of other needs deeply rooted in the
public self that do as much to obstruct what we seek as
anything outside of us can possibly do.

To fall prey to image-making dooms us to the loss of
the true self. To be accepted, to be approved, we bear
the loss of psychological freedom and call the store-
bought decisions we make our own. Until. Until they
wear out in life. Until we can't make them fit anymore.
Until the part of us that is true cries out for liberation
so loudly there is no possible way to ignore it anymore.
Then we either break our chains or break down under
them.

Choosing to be myself—to think my own thoughts, to make my own choices, to choose my own path, to take my own public positions—may risk me the Good Housekeeping seal of approval from those who want their own decisions confirmed by me. But it also gets me my most important possession—my self. "Everybody," Shirley Abbott wrote, "must learn this lesson somewhere—that it costs something to be what you are."

We live in a world that talks about individualism and then expects everyone to conform—in styles, in priorities, and in ideas. Nevertheless, it is the personal development of the self which, in the end, really enriches a society. "To be nobody but yourself in a world which is doing its best, night and day, to make you everybody else," e. e. cummings wrote, "means to fight the hardest battle which any human being can fight; and never stop fighting."

Clearly, the central question of life may be Why am I trying so hard to be what everyone else expects of me rather than what my best self expects of me? And just as important, What is the cost to everyone else of my doing it? Of my not becoming who I want to be? Who I am at the very center of my self? Who the world needs me to be?

At the end of the day, at the end of every decision, the measurement criteria must always be whether what I am doing is serving my false self or my true self, my public self or my private self. Because at the end of the day, wherever we are, whatever we choose to do at this significant plateau in life, the self is always the greatest strength, the greatest gift we have to give. If we do that, it is then that the call is heard and the gift can be given.

> *Rest not! Life is sweeping by; go and dare before you die.*
> *Something mighty and sublime, leave behind to conquer time.*
>
> GOETHE

5.

LEARNING TO HEAR THE CALL

*"I wish I could figure out what I'm really
supposed to do in life. It isn't that I don't like
the way things are now; it's just that it's not
enough."*

*"What are you talking about? Just be
happy with it. You have a great life; enjoy!"*

Life is one great and endless labyrinth. It is a puzzle
and a mystery. The need to wind our way through it,
from one unknown to the other, is fair enough. It could
even be an absorbing activity by virtue of its very ab-
struseness, if it weren't for the fact that my life is the
maze and I am the mystery.

We are all on our way to somewhere, however un-
defined, however unconscious. Without really knowing it, perhaps, we spend our days looking for the way
out of the maze of indecision, of discomfort, of unfin-
ishedness that can so easily become the soul's permanent residence. We struggle for the way to an egress

that is not there. We live looking for the something that beckons but is not clear. Why? Because we can feel it within us, that's why. It never quiets; it never sleeps. It just keeps urging us on. But to where? Answer: to nowhere I know, to do nothing I can see right now. Sometimes closer than others, always tantalizing, always just out of reach; the feeling of being in the wrong place gets so strong it can be painful.

The problem is that without clear intention, without ever stopping long enough to determine where we will end up if we stay on the road we're on now, the purpose of life can sink into the routine of routine and little more. We simply go along, turning with the turns in the road but never plotting a course of our own. Never facing the single greatest question of life: Why was I born? Meaning, what am I meant to be? What was I made to do?

If those questions are never dealt with, never answered, then we may be breathing but we are not fully alive.

If we never really face the question of where we're headed in life—and whether where we're headed is really where we want to go and are equipped to go—we are doomed to wander our way through life in some kind of empty haze. Oh, of course, my life is good, I know—but something is missing. Yes, life is even exciting, of course—but, at the same time, there is nothing more boring than excitement. Life has got to be about more than that.

It is precisely that realization, however, that discomfort, that sense of irritating void in the very center of our hearts that is, at base, the interior echo of an unanswered call to meaningfulness in life. When we are uncomfortable enough, unresigned enough, to continue to be what we are, we are finally ready to take another step through the maze of our life that leads to happiness. It is the beginning of the finding of the true self.

The choices are obvious: we can stay where we are, in the midst of our discomfort, and make do with the life that is apparently not enough for us. Or we can begin to examine the plans and projects we have already watched come to nothing in our life in order to discover what it is in all of these that is alike. Then, when we know what is not working for us, we may be able to give ourselves permission to look elsewhere, in some other category of life entirely, perhaps, in order to begin to move in other directions with fresh hope and new energy.

The world is full of financiers who quit to become artists, and lawyers who left law firms to become teachers, and CPAs who quit offices to become farmers, and teachers who left classrooms to become social workers. We all have friends who began the walk through the maze of their lives somewhere other than where they ended up. Mazes are like that. They send us off down wrong directions and then force us to try one dead end after another until suddenly the way out of nowhere becomes startlingly clear.

How else does anyone find their way to the end of a labyrinth except by trial and failure? It is, in fact, the labyrinth itself that is both the lesson and the end of life. Only by pursuing what does not fit can we ever appreciate what does.

At the same time, if we are ever to reach our particular call to completeness, to wholeness, to the true self in life, we must bring to the darkness of the maze three major characteristics.

We must come to understand that the residual dissatisfaction with life as we have shaped it for ourselves is the very essence of what we name call. Clearly, it is at the moments of dissatisfaction with what life as we know it now that the door to the future swings open for us. There is something missing in the making of who we are meant to be that we are being goaded to pursue.

Openness of heart and abandonment of soul are portals to the future. Unless I am capable of letting go of the security level to which I have become accustomed, unless I am ready to begin again, the lack of a sense of meaning in the here and now that plagues us with the grace of doubt will die in the wind. And with it will go all the unfinished parts of ourselves, left to shrivel in the face of opportunities not taken. These are the kinds of moments people look back on years later and sigh, "if only . . ." while the heart beats slower and the present loses another layer of glow.

But openness and letting go are not enough. There

is a parallel project that comes with the call to begin our lives again and that is the task of learning what we do and do not now know. Everything we have ever done has taught us something about our skills and taught us about ourselves, as well—our personality, our soul style, our dreams deferred. Simply put, there are things we may feel we are called to that we are not emotionally equipped to handle.

I talked to a young woman who loved her work, for instance. She was a documentary film editor. Making films, she told me, was her way of changing the world, of helping people to see what was going on around them so that change could come. She spent her entire working life measuring time at thirty video frames a second. A second. She was quick-fingered, intense, and precise. "Does your boyfriend work in the studio, too?" I asked, assuming that a life spent at that pace of intensity needed a partner who understood the stress of it. "Oh, no," she said, "he's an archaeologist." An archaeologist? I thought. An archaeologist measures time in eons, not in milliseconds. How would that work? I wasn't surprised to hear later that the couple had split up. He was always late for everything, her friend told me, and he never even understood why it bothered her. She interpreted his lateness as disinterest in her and her needs. Every argument they had was about time, her friend told me.

I couldn't help but wonder if, after the breakup, either of them had bothered to sit down and identify what they had learned about themselves—not necessarily about their partner—that ought to influence their choice of future partners.

To really understand what it is in life that we're looking for, we have to come to understand ourselves. Otherwise, we run the risk of making the same mistaken choices over and over and over again. Then what happens to the pursuit of happiness is the stuff of tragedy. Then what happens to the wholeness for which the human being is destined is at most a feeling of life deferred. Most of all, what happens to becoming what we were born to be goes to dust when we go on ignoring what we do or do not have to bring to it.

No authentic call is a call to more of ourselves than we have to offer.

Finally, following the call within to the world outside ourselves takes courage. It demands, too, a deep faith in the fact that there is nothing that can happen to us in the process that will do anything other than teach us more or bring us closer to our true selves. What can possibly be bad about either of those things? Clearly, failure is not failure unless we make it so.

The problem is that there are two faces of failure—one of them life-giving, the other one deadly. I have seen them both.

The first face of failure I saw in the life of an internationally recognized writer who, first intent on becoming an English professor, studied at Oxford but failed the final exam. I gasped at the very thought of it.

That, I knew, would have dashed the dreams of many against the rock of life. But she spoke about the loss of those years and that degree with a laugh and a toss of her head: "Luckiest thing that ever happened to me," she said. "Otherwise I'd be in a small college some-place teaching writing. As it is, I'm doing just what I'm supposed to be doing, writing and researching." I thought about that remark for days. Here was a woman who knew the place of failure in our eternal spiritual quest to become the best of ourselves.

The second face of failure I saw in a woman with great musical talent who, discouraged by the difficulty of her early studies, dropped out of music school and never studied another thing in life. She died disgrun-tled, underdeveloped, and trapped within the bound-aries of the self.

Clearly, failure may, in the long run, be the only real key to success, the real test of what it takes to fol-low our real call.

What is defeat? Nothing but education;
nothing but the first step to something better.
WENDELL PHILLIPS

6.

WHAT DOES IT MEAN
"TO HAVE A PURPOSE"?

*"It's not easy to know what you're
supposed to be doing in life."*
*"Maybe not, but first you have to care
enough to wonder."*

"Happiness," Helen Keller wrote, "is not attained
through self-gratification, but through fidelity to a worthy purpose." In a society bent on individualism, the
insight bends the mind a bit. But think a minute. To
realize what great stream of life flows in us, to discover
who and what we are and then to give ourselves over
to the energy and drive of it for the sake of the world
at large has got to be the greatest personal insight in
life. I knew, for instance, at the age of fourteen, that I
lived to write, was meant to write, and that life would
never be whole for me without it. I also knew, feared,
intuited that I had not the remotest notion of how to
make that happen. I was female to begin with, and it

was perfectly obvious to me, given the fact that my high school library carried books by only three women authors, that women did not write. More than that, I was going to a monastery in a male church that may have canonized women but certainly did not look to them as authors.

It was a glorious—and a painful—revelation. What do we do with something like that? With the limitations that come built right into life. For women, of course. For minorities surely. For working-class dreamers with no membership at the country club, no connections from college to ease their way from one path to another through life? Then what? Is the dream of becoming myself only for those who have the status, the resources, the time to indulge themselves in the search?

Life has changed over the last fifty years, true. Things have certainly changed in this society. But, in fact, in many ways, life seems just as limiting.

It's not so easy anymore for anyone to take for granted that we will be able to find any position in life, let alone the great soul work we think we're called to do. At the same time, it's also more likely that we will assume that anything that comes along is what we're supposed to be doing in life just because we're desperate for a job. As if a job and what we're really supposed to be doing with our lives were the same thing.

Once the banks failed and the housing market collapsed and the hedge funds dried up and Wall Street and its creative bookkeeping systems were exposed, nothing any of us had become accustomed to taking for granted has been quite the same. College is more expensive to come by. Companies have been down-sized. Venture capital has sunk. Grants and scholar-ships and benefits and student aid and social service programs have all shrunk some, if not disappeared.

We all think differently now, from one end of the economic spectrum to the other, from the CEO who once took profit for granted to the busboy who used to be able to take a job for granted. Boundlessness has vanished; limitation has set in.

We see the world differently. We see ourselves dif-ferently. The world as we knew it, with all its security, all its options, has simply disappeared. The world we had come to assume would be there forever has simply disappeared. And with it the jobs and houses and lux-ury vacations and never-ending opportunities to get on the economic escalator to get even more of them. The loss of all those things, so suddenly, so globally, so definitively, has shaken the foundations of society, of course, and yet not all of it may be as bad in the long run as it feels in the present.

Five years ago, for instance, a generation raised on the myth of interminable possibility was being told by life coaches that to be valuable in this society they needed to be able to show a minimum of five different employment positions on their résumés by the time they were forty.

The purpose, of course, was to show flexibility. But with the advent of permanent flexibility went the security of stability, the virtue of settling down somewhere or settling into the long, slow process of building a new world rather than simply expecting to find it. The very notion of being in a thing for the long haul was so dull, "so yesterday."

That generation learned to move from one thing to another, simply waiting for the big opportunity to present itself—as everyone knew that it surely would, of course.

Then, people knew, their purpose in life would be clear. Their passions satisfied.

Their happiness secured.

But the social by-product of such a worldview became very clear very soon. There was no reason in such a world to get too serious about anything too quickly. To think too hard or too much about what we were really called to—made for—in life was unnecessary. It was, of course, a dream job somewhere doing just what we wanted to do—with advancement, with perquisites, with security. We'd find it, eventually. Or better yet, it would find us. It was, far too often, in fact, all about us. The Infinite Culture had trained us for that.

We became a society that learned to try things and move on.

That kind of freewheeling, open-ended, unlimited-opportunity approach to life was a far cry from the era before it.

Before the years of spiraling stock markets and apparently endless expansion, getting into high school depended on knowing in grade school what you wanted to be in life. You had three choices. You could take a general course, a business course, or an academic course. But only an academic program qualified a person to seek a college degree. Which meant, of course, that it immediately limited your options in later life if, as a fourteen-year-old, you chose instead to take general or business courses in high school.

Life in a limited environment is more about making a living than changing the world. But not for all. In this social and economic climate, the professions became a new kind of call to social nobility. Doctors, lawyers, and teachers, like clergypersons in the eras before them, had a lofty purpose that was educationally defined and clearly delineated from the rest of humanity whose basic function was to make a living, to raise a family, to get by.

Now again, in our own time, for the first time in years, many are lucky just to get a job—and keep it. But, at the same time, it is a clarifying moment. It is more obvious than ever now that the noble purpose of life has got to be about more than simply getting the next available job. Now, it is clear, a person's purpose in life is greater than, requires more than, the ability to make money. It is also clear, then, that success in life is not limited to the successful.

We have to learn in an era such as this to weigh our

gifts against our opportunities, our needs against our demands, our emotional dreams against our material expectations. Now we need, first, to find out who we are—what are our talents and where do we find the sacred ecstasy of the soul. Then, second, we must find the work, the life, the activities that fit it. We can't drift anymore—waiting to simply slide into the next best thing in life. Now we need to find out what we love in life and work at it until it teaches us everything we have to learn from it, until we can give it back to a world in need of it more honed, more meaningful than ever.

For some it means reading to children in the local library after work at night. For others it is delivering meals-on-wheels to the homebound elderly or used furniture to the needy. For many it is in joining watch-dog groups in local communities to bring order to the streets and honesty to government. To still others, it lies in volunteering in hospitals and schools and prisons and public service agencies; to supervising neighborhood playgrounds; to participating in local ecology and housing programs; to entertaining in homes for the aged and at ethnic food fairs. Whatever it is, it is about using our own gifts to gift our world so that all of us together, our part of the human community, can have a better, happier life. And these things are waiting to be done by all of us, at every point on the social spectrum, at every economic level.

One thing is finally clear: merely having a job that

buys a house and puts a second car in the garage does not describe the limits of anyone's purpose in life.

Life can be pleasant and privileged and prestigious. But that is not enough. The truly happy life, the philosophers tell us, is about activity. Not just any activity. Not just activity that keeps us busy or has the appearance of importance. The truly happy life is about activity that gives a sense of purpose to life. It is, in other words, activity the intent of which is to do good—to go beyond our own interests and claims—to the needs of the world around us.

If we ever want to be happy, then, we need to move beyond the level of simple material satisfaction to the development of the spiritual dimension of what it means to be human. We not only need to find out what we do best and do it to the utmost. We also need to ask ourselves again why we were born. What is it that we have that the world needs and is waiting for us to provide?

That is the star we must follow to its end. Then we will not only hear the silent applause of all those who have benefited from our having lived, but we will also find the whole of ourselves now wholly developed, waiting for us, as well.

Happiness is not about money. It is about who we are and what we do with our life for the sake of the rest of the world. We need to learn that giving ourselves to something worth doing is more important, more valuable, than giving ourselves only until something better, something more exciting, something more lucrative comes along.

We need to learn to lose ourselves in what we were born to be in order to become something more than simply all the trappings of self. Then we will have become completely human. Then we will have come to be about something more than the baubles of life which, without a sense of purpose, will soon begin to define us.

The great use of life is to spend it for
something that will outlast it.

WILLIAM JAMES

7

PURPOSE AND PASSION:
THE ESSENCE OF CALL

*"What do you mean there is a woman
in the logging area hugging a tree? What in
heaven's name is she doing there!"*

*"She says, sir, that she is saving the
forest."*

It's easy to get swept away from our own best interests,
from the passions that captivate our souls and drive our
energies, in the surge of popular excitement for something else. It's also common. Tasks of the day consume
us. Schedules to which we are beholden, most of them
more polite appearances than the fruits of personal
passion—the social events, the company conferences,
the local club, the endless expectations overwhelm us.
There are simply too many of them, we argue.

But the fundamental fact of the matter may well
be that there is too little focus in me rather than too

many demands around me. I flit from one thing to another. I like to tell myself that I do it because I have multiple interests when the truth is that I have never really cultivated any of them with real depth, with real unremitting interest. If I want to know what my passion is, the question is a simple one. The question is, What do I care about? What do I care about enough to pursue it avidly, to make room in my life for it, to do something about it?

Or to put it another way, do I care about anything at all? The loss of trees, the fate of beaten children, the role of whales in the ecosystem, the continuing, increasing slaughter of civilians around the globe, destitution in my hometown, wage discrimination in the office, the declining state of education, corruption in civil government, the care of the elderly, nursing home standards? What? Am I really alive to the world around me or am I just going through the motions of being alive? Doing things but not doing much of anything significant. Engaged in activity, yes, but not in the kind of "virtuous activity" Aristotle says is the essential dimension of the happy life.

I know someone who keeps separate recycling bins for everything in the house: for plastics and metal and paper and glass. That's passion.

I know someone else who, for years and years, has circulated newspaper articles to everyone she knows in order to keep them educated to the fact that it is civilians, not soldiers, who are really dying in the wars governments devise to "protect" them. I have felt her passion touch mine.

I heard of a woman who volunteers to train one service dog after another so that wheelchair patients can live independent lives. I learned from that kind of sensitivity to be more focused on the immediate myself.

I knew a chemist in a small town that offered very little to engage children when school was out and most working-class parents were still at work. So, after work, he coached grade school Little League teams all his life just to keep those kids off the streets. Because of him, I became more adept at seeing society at all its levels rather than simply my own.

I remember the very moment I myself began to understand what people meant when they talked about systemic degradation. "This child," the TV ad said, "is handicapped." Then the camera focused in on a beautiful, curly-headed blond child squealing with delight in a field of daisies. "Handicapped? Handicapped how?" I thought. Just then the narrator's voice intoned quietly, "She's a girl," and the camera scrolled statistic after statistic across the screen. Girls/females, the figures read, are paid less, promoted less, educated less, fed less, murdered more, and beaten and raped every two minutes everywhere in the world, including in the United States of America.

I remember watching an old man outside my house

comb the street every day, forking up garbage into a black plastic bag to keep the neighborhood clean, to make our street in the inner city a decent place to live.

Suddenly I knew that just calling myself religious, just praying my prayers, just going dutifully to a class-room every day was simply not enough. Passion set in. In an instant I set out to confront the oppression of women in every action of my life wherever it was on the globe. As far as my voice could reach.

What is passion? It is what I care about enough to spend my life doing something so that someone else's life can be better because of it.

Passion is intoxicating. It gives us a reason to get up in the morning that is so meaningful, so intense that it drives us to press on from failure to failure, to tran-scend the routines of the daily for the sake of some-thing big enough to make living a gift rather than an exercise in self. "We should employ our passions in the service of life," Sir Richard Steele wrote, "not spend life in the service of our passions."

The problem, as Steele so deftly unmasks it, is that passion takes two distinct forms.

One kind of passion emerges out of a vision of life that is all consuming. The other kind of passion is ad-diction. The difference between the two is that addic-tions destroy us and vision enlarges us in mind, heart, and soul.

Addictions reduce us to a self-centeredness that

like acid—like a virus of the soul—eats us up until we die to life long before we have the grace to really die. They leave us empty of soul and broken in body. Captive to addictions, life narrows to the point that we begin to exist from one dose to the next. We become the smoker who leaves the room in the middle of significant conversations because the next cigarette is more important than the feelings or ideas of the people involved. We discover that we are the drinker who closes the bar. We become the successful lawyer who stays in the office to bill more hours rather than going home to cook a meal, or doing homework with the children, or having friends in for cards. We turn into the financier who sits at a computer long into the night willing the stock market to rise.

It's this kind of passion that shrinks our emotions and shrivels our sensitivity to anything beyond ourselves. Most of all, our addictions threaten to sour the lives of those around us. Of those closest to us. Of those who have the right to expect the most from us. Of those who have already given some part of their own lives to support and enable our own.

That's one kind of passion. The kind that harms the soul and kills the body and destroys the very capacity for love in us because it leads us to love no one but ourselves.

Those are the kinds of passion that may find us a job but that cannot give us the sense of purpose the soul seeks by which to measure the impact of its own humanity. Those passions neither enlarge our vision of life nor develop depth of soul in us. On the contrary.

Real passion, the kind that raises us to heights of soul we never knew we had, magnetizes us. It grips our imagination and touches our hearts. It is the idea that won't go away. It is the awareness that stretches us in the process.

Real passion focuses our efforts. It becomes the compass needle of the heart which presented with multiple options becomes the direction we take at every fork in the road. We are going somewhere now, not simply waiting for something to go by.

Passion both stretches us beyond ourselves and deepens us within at the same time. What we care about sets us aflame with the fire it ignites in the heart of us. It demands that we learn more and more and more. It enables us to see more and more and more. It moves us, the more we commit ourselves to its service, to do more and more and more.

We become alive with a life greater than our own and fulfilling of our own at the same time.

It's easy to talk about all the things that need to be done; it's far more difficult to figure out how I can begin to do something, however small, about it. Most of the food banks of the world are run by volunteers and a huge number of people are still alive because of them. The situation is clear: passion, you see, is not a job; it's the juice, the perfume, the electricity of life.

*There can be no happiness if the things we
believe in are different from the things we do.*

FREYA STARK

8.

WHY DOES IT TAKE SO LONG TO FIND OUT WHO I AM?

"You're thirty-five years old and you still
don't know what you really want to do in life?
When I was your age, I had already been
married and with the company for ten years."

"But when you were my age there were a
lot fewer things to choose among, to try out,
to consider."

It takes a while to learn it, but the point gets clearer by the year: life is the vessel we have been given in order to find out what life is really meant to be about.

People grow and people change. Or maybe "develop" is a better word. Or perhaps "grow into themselves" is the best of all. I know a woman, for instance, who graduated from law school and then went into psychotherapy. I know another one who became a bird breeder and then put it all down to become a nurse. I know a man who dabbled for years—a stint in construction, a couple years in sales—and then suddenly got up one morning, went to school, and became an English teacher for the rest of his life. I watched a woman science teacher suddenly quit everything and become a pharmacist in her fifties.

That kind of information simmered inside of me for years. Its lesson was not only exciting, it was fast becoming more commonplace than ever. Life is not neat, we know now, no matter how much we try to make it so. In fact, it is less neat now than ever before.

Not too long ago, getting a college degree was an exercise in meeting department requirements, lining up the necessary courses, and counting credits till graduation day. Everyone who went to college wanted to be something—a math teacher, a biologist, an engineer, a social worker, something—and quickly. Last month I asked a bright young man what he had majored in at college and his answer was as clear a piece of data about the nature of this changing world as any pictures I've ever seen from the Hubble telescope: "I don't really know what it turned out to be in the end. I think it was either biology or business economics. I never actually counted up the credits to see."

Clearly, with a few obvious exceptions like medicine, law, and computer science, the future does not now depend for most people on the turn of a couple academic credits. After all, if anything's missing that you really need, you can probably make it up online. Later.

The whole process is more a symptom, an icon of the character of modern life than it is a description of the professional fluctuations of the time. Today's world is not gained whole and entire by anybody anymore. Life in this society comes in stages, all of them discrete, all of them partial, all of them "to be continued."

Young people, for instance, put off school to go around the world. After all, they have lots of time, they figure, to look for something permanent when the backpacking is over. Or they put off commitment in order to work in another country. Or they put off settling down into any one place or position in order to get married first. Or they get a degree and then put off looking for a job in the field in which they graduated because they just stumbled into a job that pays more money and, they'll tell you, will be good experience for them anyway.

This generation, in fact, seems to know intuitively what past generations only found out later: Being twenty-one is not the acme of life. Life is not finished then. Exploration does not end then. In fact, it has barely begun.

It's a long meandering road, this journey to human completion, to the point where all the possible roads in life—personal, social, emotional, spiritual—converge at the same center. It's a moment to be dearly sought after, but it is seldom arrived at without a number of twists and turns along the way. Life itself, in fact, is the process of putting all the pieces together.

The notion that we can become all that we're meant to be, all at the same time, all instantly, all at once, without bungling along as we go, is pure fantasy. Or to put it another way, the notion that we can make great life decisions once and for all without learning as we go is pure naïveté. Life is not a paint-by-numbers game.

In the first place, some parts of us simply mature faster than others. Intellectually, for instance, we may be wizards. There's not a test they ever gave us that we failed. But emotionally, we stayed teenagers till we were forty. In fact, we are still inclined to cry or throw temper tantrums or go into depression over small slights or major differences of opinion. Or perhaps emotionally we're wise beyond our years, but we didn't even begin to take intellectual development seriously until we were over thirty.

So what hope is there for finding out what we are really meant to do in life if we ourselves are simply a confluence of distinctly developing systems, all of them at different times, none of them completely independent of the others?

The fact is that fullness of life is not the result of any single decision or move or job or interest. It is an amalgam, I think, of all the streams of reality that lie in the undercurrent of what it means when we say that we're happy:

First, I need to be very clear that real happiness, according to Aristotle, depends on the full development of the self, physically, emotionally, spiritually. It means more than pleasure, though pleasure is certainly important in life. It means doing the best we can in whatever we do and living with purpose wherever we are. It means having a sense of aim and direction, of resolve and intent. It means developing all of our abilities to the utmost and using them well. It means being fully alive. It means, surely, what Jesus meant when he said, "What does it profit a person to gain the whole world and lose their lives?" Sometimes "the shortest distance between two points," at least in matters of the soul, the spirit, and the fullness of the self, may well be a very circuitous route.

Second, we can never be happy as long as we confuse pleasure and happiness. One more car, the long trip, night after night on the town, one instantaneous gratification after another are no substitute for doing something purposeful in life. We can go only so many miles in our new car until it gets to be an old car. We can travel only so far. We can only sit on a sundeck so long till sitting there is more of an irritation than a joy. Then we have to start all over to amuse ourselves when we should be developing ourselves.

Third, we must realize that real happiness depends on our making some genuine contribution to life, on doing something that makes life better not only for ourselves but for others as well.

Fourth, we must become actively engaged in the kinds of things that serve whatever we define as the overarching purpose or service or passion of our lives, if not through the work we do then through the activities in which we engage. The S.O.N.S. (Save Our Native Species), for instance, are avid fisher folk who banded together to save the local lake and its species rather than fish the lake out. The Inner-City Neighborhood Art House is a place where the artists of the area teach young people of the inner city painting, drawing, music, crafts, and dance tuition-free so that the soul of the city does not die where the city needs soul most. The Erie Community Foundation is the place where philanthropists of the region pool their resources to support local projects that benefit the entire city—such as mobile libraries and soup kitchens and neighborhood rehabilitation programs. Point: Life is not an exercise for casual bystanders. Unless we are involved, neither we nor the world can become all that we are meant to be.

Fifth, we must come to understand that life is not a destination; it is a process of bringing to completeness all the gifts we have been given. It is an exercise in discovering our gifts and how to give them.

We are what we are. But the gift of self unfolds as we go, often slowly, always with surprise. It can take years before the real gift that is hidden within us becomes clear. Which is why so few people really stay in the areas for which they were prepared as children and students.

In the end, then, it is imperative that we be patient

with ourselves as we grow. What we want to do and are meant to do will emerge. Eventually. It comes to life in us as we go. It becomes clear in little bits of ourselves what we do not want to be, let alone in glimpses of the grayed-out life we seek. It shows itself, as well, out of the unknown parts of ourselves that are often discovered only by necessity. We must simply keep moving in the direction of happiness—in pursuit of our passions and in our commitment to determining their purpose—and one day it will happen in us before we even realize that happiness has come.

Enough shovels of earth, a mountain.
Enough pails of water, a river.
CHINESE PROVERB

9.

WHAT IS A GIFT?

"You are the best cook I know. You should be doing something in that field."
"Oh, for heaven's sake, if you can read, you can cook. Anybody can cook."

David was a very bright, very nervous, very introverted little guy with a very smooth-talking, outgoing, self-confident older brother. Michael, the brother, became a rabbi at an early age and moved quickly into a large congregation with a national reputation.

David, on the other hand, had little to no interest in school, however much his parents tried to tell him that he was even brighter than his brother had been. In fact, David's grades, except in his foreign language courses, were barely more than average, and his social interests were even lower. Most of the time he simply retreated into his bedroom to surf the Net or read books in one language or another. He couldn't get a job and he didn't want to go to college, he said.

By the time his mother told me about him, David was in his midtwenties and the parents were beside themselves with worry. Why was it that this boy of all boys could not see his own talent? She was doing everything she could to lead him to trust his own ability, but nothing seemed to work. How could that possibly be? she wanted to know.

The answer was an easy one to overlook. David's problem was not that he was not gifted. David's problem was that he was. Languages came naturally to him. Naturally. Unlike most, he did not struggle to memorize verbs or do translations. He simply knew how to do it. Languages came to him like ether in air. He took Spanish in high school, of course, but after that, he simply began to teach himself the rest of the languages—one after another after another. But, at the same time, he didn't study much of anything else. In other subjects his grades declined. How, as his mother said, could that possibly be?

The problem is that people who are unusually gifted in something often tend to take it for granted. They got it without effort, after all, so everyone else must have it, too, right? In fact, they are often inclined not only to discount the gift itself as commonplace or even worthless but to doubt their own abilities in anything else. What they do know, they know intuitively, after all, rather than by dint of great effort, so are they capable of learning anything else or not? The gift in them, that is so clearly striking to everyone else, is, ironically, invisible to them.

And yet it is exactly what we are inclined to overlook in ourselves that is often our greatest asset.

I knew a very talented musician who played multiple musical instruments by ear. She arranged songs in five-part harmony in her head. She wrote all the parts of her first symphony at a dining room table. And yet she never heard those parts aloud herself until it was performed in public by the local symphony orchestra. Nevertheless what she knew best about herself was not what she could do in music, but what she could not do, however much people affirmed her great talent. In fact, because she played everything by ear she did not read music comfortably. Just as great writers are not always great speakers, what she could not do was to confine herself to any given piece of music without embellishing it, adding layers to its harmony, arpeggios to its rests. So she refused to accompany the chorus if she had not practiced the piece beforehand. Her fear was that she would move away from the sheet music in front of her and play instead the arrangement for it that flowed unedited through her head. Even other musicians failed to understand that there was a curse as well as a blessing to her giftedness.

Our gifts—the things we do best, the things we do with almost no effort, the talents in us that we take for granted—can both consume us and mislead us. They are the magnets that captivate us and they are, at the same time, the shell that conceals us from ourselves.

But these special parts of ourselves—and we all have them, in something, to some degree—are what make us who we are. They cannot be ignored because they are the parts of us that lie in waiting within us, just waiting to break out into the uniqueness that is ourselves.

To be gifted does not mean to be a genius; it means to have some singular ability to an unusual degree. It's what we do to an accomplished level, almost without thinking. It's the woodworker who becomes a restorer. Or a welder whose welds are invisible. Or the receptionist who makes everyone who walks in the door feel at home. A young girl I know with Down syndrome was hired to do run-and-fetch work around the office. To the astonishment of everyone but herself, she became its most proficient, most intense, most responsible file clerk. She loved to put things in order, and she did it with all her heart. To her it was a great, Olympian victory to put a cryptogram of printed materials into the right file folder in the right drawer. It was not a dull and agitating routine. Her gift was a gift to the whole system. Its value to her sense of human development and to the efficiency of the operation itself lay in her being able to recognize it and accept it.

Gifts are those precious parts of ourselves that lurk in the depths of us just waiting to be given away. Just looking for a place to burst open. Just wishing for the chance and the time and the encouragement and the opportunity to blossom in the bright light of humanity.

They niggle at the heart of us during the day and plague our sleep at night. "What do you think about when you're not throwing pots?" I asked an artist. "The pots I will throw tomorrow," he said.

One thing we know about gifts: gifts will out. Whether we acknowledge them or not, whether we develop them or not, whether we honor them in our daily lives or not, they simply emerge in us. Gifts have a way of showing up where and when they're least expected in life: like the long-haul truck driver who frames photos in his basement. Or the nurse who collects antique jewelry on the weekends. Or the accountant who volunteers to teach crippled children how to ride a horse.

Gifts are contributions to the livability of life that we simply cannot not share with others. Positive psychologists tell us that one of the unfailing ways to identify our own gifts is to begin to notice what it is that moves us into an emotional zone beyond consciousness of time. When is it that we say with total honesty and simplicity, "I had no idea that it was already midnight when I stopped knitting."

I remember the Saturdays I couldn't wait to get into the small darkroom to develop and print the film I'd shot during the week. I loved the smell of the chemicals and the soft red light and the sight of the black-and-white print emerging in the swirling waters of the tray of developing fluid. In that room all time stopped for me. There was only one thing driving the work: the sheer giddy joy of producing what my mind had created and the knowledge that this exercise in getting something out of nothing would appear in the next issue of the little magazine I loved. My professional education was in other things, but it was giving expression to the ink in my veins that really touched the *me* in me.

A gift is a very personal part of us. It's special. It taps in us what nothing else in life can even begin to explore. And yet so many of us make so little of our gifts, consider them "hobbies" more than specialties, go so far sometimes as even to hide them from public sight. But it is in our giftedness that our future lies. To be really happy, we must either follow our gifts or find our gifts. Otherwise we run the risk of going to our graves only half alive.

When we finally take that first step toward being honest about what we ourselves really believe, really want to do, really enjoy most, are really most committed to doing for others—and do it—we become a person who is a gift to the rest of the human race. Then the wisdom in us becomes a benefice to the rest of the world. Then we come closer to being our own true selves.

I'll walk where my own nature would be
  leading;
It vexes me to choose another guide.

EMILY BRONTË

life, to prove that there really was a way to get to the east by going west.

It's impossible to imagine what would have happened to the science of evolution and our understanding of the development of life if it had not been for the painstaking collection of fossils—tiny fragments of bone and skull that finally proved the interconnectedness of the animal and human kingdom—thanks to paleontologists throughout the world. Most of them were derided as fools or rejected as atheists. Yet, following the light within them, they nevertheless could not stop themselves from going on despite it all.

And, frankly, it's equally impossible to think of my own life—and yours, too, I'm sure—and not find that it has been made up of two equal parts—one part a persistent pursuit of our secret loves, the other part surprise at the reactions of those with whom we finally shared it. In what life are there not the ecstasy and agony, the determinations and surprises that mark our own excursions in search of the fullness of ourselves?

It's so easy to take for granted all the great thinkers like Einstein, inventors like Marconi, scientists like Teilhard de Chardin, writers like Lewis Carroll, and artists like Georgia O'Keeffe who worked at one thing but all the while kept following the dream in them of something better until, finally, it became the fullness of their lives, as well.

These are the ones who make the world a living,

10.

WHY FOLLOW THE GIFTS?

"If you like to do that, why don't you do more of it?"

"Because everybody says it's a waste of time."

Life is full of people who have felt a drive in them that few, if any, felt they should follow.

I never board a plane without remembering that people laughed at the Wright Brothers, almost hooted them out of town, in fact, for thinking that human beings could possibly fly.

It's difficult to walk into a voting booth and not remember the women who were arrested outside the White House and force-fed in a Washington jail to break the hunger strikes they waged so that I could vote.

It's hard to travel around the world and not think of Christopher Columbus who spent his life, risked his growing, exciting place for the rest of us to be. These are the ones who refuse to quit until the song of their lives matches the song of their hearts.

When we, you and I, do that, too, then everything fits. Everything is right. Everything feels complete in us.

The fact is that every one of us has a life to live that is right for us and a light to others at the same time. Sometimes our jobs and our gifts come together; sometimes we work to live at one and live to work at the other.

There are those, of course, who are never happy with their own gifts and would prefer instead the gifts they see around them. Whatever they are, they want to be something else. They are the great composer Salieri who wanted to be the pianist Mozart. They are inspired actors who want to be directors. They are inspiring English teachers who want instead to be writers. And all of them spend life struggling with whether they have the capabilities to be other than they are or not.

It is a sad and self-destructive situation, this rejection of the self for the sake of some totally unattainable self-image.

But there are those who have learned to accept themselves to the hilt, to be comfortable with who they are, and to value the gifts they have rather than devalue themselves on the basis of the gifts they lack.

Theirs are the gifts that make the world better for everyone else. Theirs are the gifts we need to complement our own. They are the people the rest of us seek out in life. The secretary who never misses a call-back notice is a gift to the world. The teacher's aide who takes extra time with a bright but frightened child is a gift to the world. The woman whose weaving is a gift to the ages is a gift to the world. The president who refuses to make war when making treaties will do is a gift to the world. The person who does not disdain to be what they are to the best of their ability is a living gift to the world.

But if that is true—and history is sure that it is—then life will not really be right for any of us until each of us discovers what it is in us that is bursting to be released. Then it is only a matter of allowing ourselves to emancipate it, to set it free in the world, to offer it to those who know somehow that they need it but do not have it themselves.

When we find that gift, that skill, that talent, that insight, that magic in ourselves, either by persistence or by happenstance, we will find the entire world waiting for it—and for us.

But, in the meantime, I know, there are great pressures to be dealt with in the process.

The very notion that anyone in this society should ever have fewer things than anyone else is, in itself, a sign of degradation. Things define us. So to pursue the development of an inner gift rather than devote ourselves to the social insignia of accumulation can be a lonely—and little appreciated—path for a while. It takes a great deal of courage to choose the way that leads to the true self rather than to submerge the self for the rest of my life in an attempt to substitute things for fullness of life.

Prestige—the choice of a position over a call to the giving of a gift that brings satisfaction far beyond what any title on any door can provide—can seduce a person. It can lure us away from the only thing in life—our own fullness of development—that can promise any kind of real happiness.

Advancement, the perpetual striving for a brass ring that shines but does not bring the kinds of value the heart seeks, is always short-lived. The promotions end; the best of public positions eventually fade or fail; the world moves on to the next puny bit of power. And then what? Then what of the self is really left to comfort us now when we're finished or out of the place or alone?

What we do best is what we are meant to do in life. That is our talent. Sometimes it has to do with ideas, sometimes it's skills, sometimes it's people. But whatever it is, we are born to find our gifts so we can then give them away. "If you are talented," Mehmet Ildan wrote, "don't sit in the darkness, light a candle so that others can see you."

The fact is that the gift within us, the one that emerges out of the center of the self, the one we were born with and which has led us from scrap to scrap of itself all our born days, is our destiny, our call. That special talent, that favorite pursuit, that most fulfilling experience, is the sum total of the real self. Some people say it's a "call," meaning an invitation to become what we were meant to be. Other people call it a "vocation," meaning an answer to the beckoning of the God who gave us a gift so that we ourselves could give it away to those who need it. Swami Raj said, "Talent—that's God's finger on the shoulder." Jesus called it "not hiding your light under a bushel."

This call, this essential self, can take years to find— or at least years to understand or to hone or to perfect. I know that's true because it happened to me. It was my first week in high school. The first-year English teacher assigned one of those summer vacation essays that have plagued every student in the world somewhere along the line. I'm sure teachers do it to determine the grammatical level of every new class as a kind of starting point for the semester's lesson plans. All I know is that I took the assignment seriously. I don't have a clue now what I wrote—only that frankly it could not have been much. My family did not take exotic vacations. I only know that the day after the assignment was due, the English teacher knocked on the door of the algebra class where I was sitting, desperately waiting for the bell to ring.

"Who wrote this, Joan?" she said.

"I did," I said, wondering if I had forgotten to put my name on the paper.

"Are you sure?" she said.

I looked over the paper for my name. "That's my name," I said, thinking that she probably couldn't put names and faces together yet.

"How much of it did your mother write?" she went on.

"My mother?" I said, shocked and embarrassed by the question. "None of it!"

She gave me a long, hard look. "In that case," she said slowly, "I want you to report to the journalism room immediately after class."

At that exact moment, my life changed forever.

I didn't really understand the full implications of that single moment, that single choice, for years. But when I look back now, I am certain that the long journey from that high school journalism room to this page of writing today begun for me then with total commitment, with full heartedness, with a sense of coming home. Finally, I knew where I was going. And though writing has never been my job, it has always been my life.

I am equally convinced that the journey is the same for most of us. Somewhere along the line, the seed is planted in us that changes us forever. The call comes, quietly and out of nowhere. Something new rises in the soul. And then it is time to answer.

*There is only one success—to be able to spend
your life in your own way.*

CHRISTOPHER MORLEY

11.

WHAT DOES IT MEAN TO HAVE A CALL?

"You're going where? To do what? For heaven's sake, why?"

"I'm not really sure. I only know that unless I try this, I'll never be happy."

Call is an awesome word. It rings of the divine and smacks of destiny: it is the thing we feel we can't avoid doing, even when we didn't want to do it in the first place. It is the concept that makes decision-making a kind of cosmic dice game, a round of hide-and-seek, as if someone somewhere knows what we are meant to do and is waiting to see if we'll get it right. And woe to us if we don't. Responsibility for what we do in life, from this point of view, falls somewhere else. Not on us.

There is no doubt, of course, that a lot of what happens to us in life seems to be happenstance, out of our control, determinative. And it is. It always has been.

Who knows when it happened? Most of us don't

even know who did it. But one thing we can be sure of: if we're where we are today—maybe even who we are today—it's because someone somewhere—a great-grandparent, a grandparent, a parent—found themselves at a turn in the road, and took it.

For some reason unknown to us, perhaps not even fully conscious to them, someone in our history found themselves at the end of one road and facing two others. Then, choosing the road on the left rather than the road on the right, they began their lives all over again. And that has made all the difference—not simply for them but for us as well.

They left Poland or Russia or Ireland or Germany or Italy or Africa or Mexico or England. Or they left a job and a state and a home. Whatever it was, they left something they had no intention of leaving long before they thought they had finished with it. Until along came the unforeseen. Along came the crossroad. At that point they left one life behind and made a new one. In most cases they weren't transported or forced; they weren't sure where the road would lead and they weren't guaranteed success. They simply knew that life for them was somewhere and something else than what they had known. They simply knew that they were un-finished and required to do something else. They knew that they had to take responsibility for their lives at a time when the future was unclear and the past was no longer the answer to it.

It is this process of taking responsibility for the ful-

fillment of our lives that is the fundamental process
of answering the call for the more that now cries for
attention within us.

Clearly, the question that lingers as a result of those
twisting, turning histories of the vagaries of our family backgrounds is a simple one: would we—can we—
make the kind of hard choices our ancestors did in
following the calls that led to the here and now of our
own lives? When faced with great decision-making
moments, can we deal with the dilemma of unsure
choices nearly as well as they did? Can we face the
dark roads and uncertain ends and the relentless summons that sound from the depth of our own souls whis-
pering to us that there is more to life for us than this?
The question is a pivotal one. There is no such thing
as one great life choice. The truth is that life is a series
of choices, some of them more major than others, but
all of them, in the end, defining.

It is this unending search for the more in life that
is of the essence of call. It is the spiritual summons to
fullness of life, to the pursuit of what is still lacking in
us, to the hope for fulfillment.

The most serious mutation in the general understanding of call may well be developing in our own
lifetime. As recently as seventy-five years ago a question about what we intended to do with our lives
was expected to be answered by adolescents. As sec-
ondary education became more and more the norm
of a person's educational history, and school became

mandatory, a high school education became the entree to an adult life less agrarian, more transient, considerably more varied than at any other time in history. Suddenly, whole populations of people, sociologists tell us, who had never ventured more than seven square miles away from home or thought of anything beyond the local or had much in the way of decisions about life choices at all, were suddenly confronted with the need to make vocational choices until then largely unheard of in the general population.

High school, an educational level for those between the ages of fourteen and seventeen, became society's ingress to adulthood, to life, to vocation. High school courses set a person's direction for life, cast their life direction in stone, shaped the very nature of their personal lives. College was a luxury for most. Money came hard and slow. Life was cheap. War was persistent. And life circled around male needs and male choices.

But the ebb and flow of history after the rise of industry, the massive social upheaval of world wars, the advent of global transportation, the coming of the computer age, and, for women, feminism, has changed the way we live life. The expectation of lifelong positions is gone and with it the certainty of lifelong living situations. We are a people in flux, a people in search of meaning in a world in global flux.

The process has been mind shattering, let alone unsettling psychologically. We are uprooted and isolated from our faraway beginnings. More, we are totally unsure of what the future will look like in a society caught between two distinctly different centuries and the distinctly different cultures they have wrought. The last century changed our lives; this one is changing our world.

One morning I got news of one cousin's death in New York from a priest cousin I have never met who lives in Italy but who is at present on short-term business in Malaysia and keeping in touch with the rest of the world on a portable computer. None of that would have been plausible until now when it has become commonplace to a class of people within reach of modern technology. But in a world like that, where change is the only stable element of the culture, how can there be such a thing as a call at all? Or, to put it another way, was there really such a thing as a call when there were few great life-changing choices for anyone?

And if so, what exactly is a call now and to what? To a job? To a new life? To a mission? To something else entirely, perhaps?

The question is a crucial one because in this culture a call comes in many guises, many times in life. In this era, and, I think, for the foreseeable future, there are at least three major decision-making points in every person's history: the first comes in early adulthood; the second at the time of midlife review; and the third at the point of later-stage transition. At each of these points, new and major decisions must be made about personal direction and personal purpose and personal happiness that may include work changes but, at base, are far, far more important than that.

My call may certainly require that I make a decision about what work I will do in life as a result of it. But changing jobs is not the only thing call is about and, in fact, may have little or nothing to do with my choice of a job at all. A number of artists—writers, painters, actors—work at one thing to survive while concentrating the energies of their souls on developing the natural gifts within them in other ways. Or, I may use my job to enable me to raise service dogs for poor children in my spare time. Or as a chemist I may take a job in one laboratory after another in order to pursue my heart's commitment to make Alzheimer's disease obsolete. Or I may use my carpentry skills to build tent houses for homeless children in Haiti. Or give my medical skills to remove cataracts in Latin America.

The important thing is to know what I want to do in life in light of both the talents I have and the cries of the world around me for help.

Some people stay on roads long gone purposeless to them because they fear the unknowns of another one—a posture far different from the pioneer families who first plowed new land to raise us. For them, change promised more security than they would have had by clinging to the familiar. For many now, however, in a culture that defines success as arriving at some pinnacle of permanent security, change is as likely to be seen as much a threat as it is an opportunity.

Some of us, on the other hand, like rolling stones, are too quick to leave a road, crossroad or not, whose only lack is that it isn't clear at the moment. For those for whom change is its own kind of elixir, simply moving to something new is more important than making life decisions that build on the past.

But most of us know when we're at a crossroad in life, when old answers have gone dry, when our souls have gone dry here, when nothing but another choice is possible. Then comes the struggle and the dickering, the pain and the fear over which of the many directions we could take, over which we ought to take.

Indeed, the big decisions in life are hardly ever clear—except for one. And that one is piercingly clear: life is a series of dilemmas, of options, of conundrums, of possibilities taken and not taken. Negotiating these moments well is of the essence of the life well lived.

As a result, we know now that this search for the whole self is no longer resolved through an educational process alone or even the choice of a good career. This search for the whole self is a process of making spiritual choices between the good and the better, the holy and the mundane, the essence of life and the cosmetic. We have built change into our futures, our educational options, our lives. We have come to understand that no life is set in stone anymore. On the contrary, life is a slow-won evolution of the self that taps every level of our lives and touches all its great questions.

Choice is the holy-making stuff of life. There is no such thing as the inconsequential. Everything we do affects something and someone. Choice, therefore, is a spiritual skill of great import.

Every action of our lives touches on some chord that will vibrate in eternity.

EDWIN CHAPIN

12.

THE FIRST CALL: AN INVITATION TO ADULTHOOD

*"What do you want to do once you're
finished with all your courses?"*

*"Well, I wanted to be a history teacher,
but my dad said he wasn't going to pay for a
degree that had no financial future. So I got a
business degree instead."*

The first great life decision, the first step on the way to
ferreting out our call in life, happens at the threshold
of adult independence. Preparation time is over now.
The shelter from career expectations enjoyed during
high school or college has ended. Life is no longer a
rehearsal for living. On the contrary. Parents step back
into the shadows a bit. Teachers disappear. Friends go
their own separate ways. Suddenly, I find that, surrounded by people, I am actually very alone. There are
bills to pay now. There are daily schedules to keep that
cannot be ignored or renegotiated any longer. There

are circumstances and situations and possibilities to consider that have never even been questions before this: Should I stay here or go there? Do this or do that? And if not that, then what? The choices are mine now. Big choices.

A lot of them, of course, we simply stumble through, making life up as we go. Or we fall into them rather than really choose them. We take an offer simply because it's there. After all, it seems there are no other clear alternatives, there is no really strong competing inclination, nothing better to do at the moment. So why not?

But those choices are often not really choices at all. Those are opportunities, fancies, lessons, experiences—all of which will hold me in good stead someday, but they are not necessarily real preferences.

It is preferences—not opportunities—which, in the end, make all the difference. Opportunities overwhelm us. But the choices we make between one preference and another are the choices that count.

The question that vibrates within us, the question that will not go away no matter how long we manage to ignore it consciously is the one that haunts us from one day, one year, one age to the other. What do I really *want* to do with my life? What am I really *meant* to do with my life?

Until we answer that question, no other question of our lives can possibly be answered well. No other answer will really satisfy. No other choices can ever really make us happy. Everything else, as responsible and dedicated and honest as we may be, is pure drift. It is finding the direction toward which the heart inclines that is the key to human fulfillment.

The problem is that we live in a culture where the voice of vocation, the magnet toward meaning, is a hard one to hear in the clamor of competing interests. The culture is full of criteria for success that have almost nothing to do with happiness, with Aristotle's notion of "virtuous activity," with the recognition that we have all been born to make the world better because we have been here. Distinguishing what we are meant to do in life from the glamour of more seductive appeals is not an easy one. The concept of finding my role in life rather than simply moving from one kind of employment to another is prey to the enticements of material success around it.

Get money, the culture demands. Or power. Or prestige, at least. Get the trappings of the good life, the rumor of the great life, the reputation of success, the culture says, and that will be enough.

But it isn't.

As a result, we are a culture of misfits—not because there is anything wrong with us as a people but because we are accustomed to becoming things we aren't. It can take years before we discover how to fit into our own souls. Our schools educate students to fit the economy, for instance, rather than to expand their hearts and seed their souls. The humanizing dimension of education—basic or core courses in the liberal arts, the history of thought, the debates of the great thinkers of the past, the dimming of ethical questions in society—get lost in the development of technical or professional skills.

So we get politicians who have never even read Dickens's *Oliver Twist* and, as a result, are blind to the tragedy of child labor in our own day. We get financiers who think that limitless profit taking makes for economic sense, ignoring the price we pay as a people when that kind of economics leaves a few at the top and the rest of the culture in shambles. We get men in every arena of state and church who take it for granted that women are for their use.

A direct corollary of that kind of thinking is obvious: We get students who go into finance rather than philosophy because accounting pays more. Fine writers go into law because law is more prestigious. Young people with artistic talent go into computer science or hotel management or engineering because these fields are full of the "opportunities"—real "money"—that a watercolorist or an ethicist lacks. It's not that accounting or law or finance or computer science are not worthy subjects. It is that in order for work to be fully worthy—to be truly a "virtuous activity"—a person must choose it for worthy reasons and use it to do worthy things.

The problem is that when we do not do what we are clearly made to do, meant to do, and what we need to do for the sake of the world as well as the security of the self, we are doomed. "The great use of life," William James wrote, "is to spend it for something that will outlast it."

It is those kinds of things—the things that make life better for everyone—that are certifiable vocations. It is those kinds of choices that are genuine life commitments, endemically holy undertakings. It is in making choices designed to make the world a more moral place, a more just and livable place, that make life worth living. It is what is undertaken because we chose to do what needs to be done rather than what is simply convenient and comfortable. It is those things that make the measure of a life.

The problem is that when we do not do what we are clearly made to do we are doomed. If the world needs interpreters of the past so that we might forge a finer future, then to forego that talent in ourselves for the sake of quick money is to betray the higher part of our own humanity. Worse, to do that is to spend the rest of our lives looking for the missing pieces of ourselves that we lost before we even knew we had them.

We lose the part of ourselves that is our most spiritual self. We become one more cog in the economic wheel that puts out products, without asking whether what we are producing is humanizing or not.

*We have to stumble through so much dirt and
humbug before we reach home.
And we have no one to guide us. Our only
guide is our homesickness.*

HERMANN HESSE

13.

THE SECOND CALL

*"I don't know what's wrong with me. I've
always been so happy. Until recently, that is.
Now all I think about is wanting to be out of
here."*

*"Don't do anything rash. These things
pass—eventually. Just ignore it."*

~

"The only man I know who behaves sensibly," George
Bernard Shaw wrote, "is my tailor; he takes my measurements anew each time he sees me. The rest go on with
their old measurements and expect me to fit them."

Sometime in the early middle of life, we wake up
one morning to discover that our measurements have
changed. What we have been doing for years, we
begin to realize, simply does not fit us anymore. We
have outgrown the young life that we thought would
go on forever and have found within us a whole new
person. Worse, we find ourselves lodged in a life we no
longer find stimulating or satisfying or exciting. We

are unfamiliar—even to ourselves. We find that we are living some kind of creeping death, sloughing off what fit us in the past, in the old life we thought we loved, and unable to find a new way to fit into our present.

The feelings that come with the realization are overwhelming. One part guilt, one part fear, they make us ill in soul. We know what we cannot admit. If we do not stay as we are, we will feel forever unfaithful. If we force ourselves to stay as we are, we will go to dust inside.

There is so much at stake now. So much life behind us has been invested in what we now find to be lifeless. And yet there is so much life left to live. How can we possibly live it like this? And where did we go wrong? What happened to our commitment to the life decision we made in an earlier life? And what is at the root of this shift of centeredness: A lack of the kind of personal responsibility that sees a thing through? Immaturity? A lack of focus? What?

And the usual answer is "none of the above."

Assuming that tomorrow will be the same as today is poor preparation for living. It equips us only for disappointment or, more likely, for shock. To live well, to be mentally healthy, we must learn to realize that life is a work in process.

"Don't worry, Joan, you will go on," a wise woman told me once, after a particularly painful period in life, "but you will go on differently now. You will, in fact, be stronger than ever before." And she was right.

The whole notion that once we make an early adult decision about what we will do with our lives we'll never make another one is pure myth, wishful thinking at best, an illusion. Everything changes as experience replaces fantasy: the way we think, the ideas we believe, the people we admire, the things we value. All of it is up for review. Some of it gets reaffirmed. Much of it gets discarded. And with it the way we lived before the great spiritual earthquake happened in us. No doubt about it: life's great decisions must be revisited again and again and again if we ever really intend to find our way from one phase to another. What else can possibly keep them fresh? What other than rethinking them can make them life-giving every day of our lives? What more than reappraising them can bring us to the fullness of them?

But those kinds of understandings—and the patience they call for—come later. After the fact. After the pain of having faced the truths that come with the unmasking of the unfinished parts of us are long gone.

The temptation, of course, is to take our first decisions for granted, to fail to see that we go on growing, changing, becoming new—even to ourselves.

Why is the realization that life is not settled yet so threatening to our sense of self, to our definition of life itself, to our hopes for the future? If there is a moment when the call to something greater than ourselves is real, this is certainly it. If anything has happened to us at all as the years went by, it is more than likely the fact that we ignored our own growing.

Instead, someplace in the course of those years, we chose static and confused it with stable. We failed to change with the changes around us that prodded change within us, as well. We ignored all the signs: the sense of emptiness, the lack of passion for anything, the frenzying pace without real purpose. Passion and purpose. Passion and purpose went to dust. And we did nothing about it. We didn't even notice it go as we sank further and further into the boredom of routine. The old activities no longer captivated either our imagination or our soul. The old canons of the meaningful life are simply no longer large enough to hold the soul that has outgrown them.

We find ourselves dissatisfied with the limits of the life we're living now. What had been good enough for us when we were younger just isn't any longer. Down deep we know that there has to be more to it than a house, a car, a job, a television set, and a gaggle of meetings to go to. There has to be something more important to do than simply get up every morning and slog through a day that once, perhaps, inebriated our souls but now only bores us to tears. As Goethe put it, "A useless life is an early death."

Dashed expectations—the images of the grandeur of personal freedom that once plagued us—have shown themselves to be neither grand nor real. Freedom, it seems, is an illusion. Whatever great and glorious things we set out to do for the world, either turned out to be less glorious than we ever thought possible, or simply are impervious to change. The world is yet to go green. The whales are still being slaughtered. Children, it seems, are more abused than ever. Women are still second-class everywhere.

With all those things, for the product-oriented, success-driven person, at least, comes emptiness. Something's missing. Something isn't working. But what is it?

We like to think that the young are restless to grow up; we fail to realize that the middle-aged are restless about it, too. But where the young are growing out of themselves to a call that beckons from beyond them, the middle-aged are growing down now, into the depth of themselves where the call is waiting to be rethought, reassessed, fulfilled. Life just goes on demanding new life from us all the time.

So what's missing? What's missing is the passion and the purpose that brought us to this point. What's missing is our dedication to something other than ourselves. Zoning out, taking what was once of greatest urgency for granted now is one thing. But settling in is entirely another. Nothing we are now—an Olympic swimmer, the chair of the board, the owner of the bank, the employee of the year, the parent of the valedictorian—will be in ten more years what it is now. When those things go, what will we be then? What will freshen the life of the heart then? The message is clear: we must each be more at all times than what we are at any given time.

The secret to life is the willingness to grow into something that is beyond our present. In middle age we must be prepared to begin again. One stage of our life work is over now, but there is so much yet to be done, and our obligation as a human being is to be an ongoing part of doing it. Despair at what has not happened is not acceptable. "No seed ever sees the flower," the Zen master teaches. We do not give ourselves to the great questions of life because we expect to solve them. We give ourselves to the adamantine, entanglements of life because we must, because to do less is to be less than fully human.

Growth is the sloughing off of the past in order to become something we never expected was possible in the stage of life before it. Whatever of our first stage of commitment has been exhausted, the call to purpose and passion goes on. And so, therefore, must we. The answer to that call in middle age is the genus of the happy life.

The seen is the changing,
the unseen is the unchanging.

PLATO

14.

THE THIRD CALL

"I hear you've retired. What will you be doing now?"

"Well, that's the problem, isn't it: What is there to do?"

At some point in time, all the cosmetics of life—titles and money, positions and schedules, civic committees and public service activities—end as quietly and unobtrusively as they began. By the time we turn in the key to the supply cupboard and leave the floor for the last time, the new name is being nailed over the door, the new filing cabinets are being rolled in, the staff is already waiting in line to see someone else for the answers that once made you important, that now make someone else important.

As the poet Robert Frost put it, "In three words I can sum up everything I've learned about life. It goes on." And that's true, of course. But not completely. And only if.

From now on, it will not go on in you with the same old identity, and it doesn't even go on at the workplace the same way. Without your experience and your institutional memory of the system and your understanding of the history of the place, it too will change. There will be a part of both of you that will be incomplete now. The difference is that the change in them will look less obvious. It will be total for you.

And yet, at the same time, this is exactly when life is meant to go on for you in a completely new way. This is when it becomes clear that what people told you for years is true: a job and a life are not the same thing. Now the question is not Is there a job for you to do? Now the question is Who are you without the job? What kind of a person have you developed into over the years, who is far and beyond the job?

The question is an important one because it is that person—the person that is the soul of you—that the world is waiting for, that the world needs now. It is time for you to hear the third phase of the call you have heard within you over the years. This stage of the call is the call to completion.

In the first stage of the call, you followed a purpose and a passion that shaped your very existence. It led you up and down the highways and byways of life— surprised you in some places by its very energy, disappointed you with its lack of final resolution. Life was more about choice then, finding the place where your abilities and your passion, your commitment and your sense of purpose could be merged. You went from one place to another, trying there, testing here, until with one last great hope, and time running out, you settled into the best of the dream you could find available.

In the second stage of the call, with your life's fulfillment in doubt and its energy low, you began to question its very validity, its worth, its reality. Searching yet for some portion of the grail of life, you changed some things and added other things and abandoned whole parts of it. Whatever it was that led you to this moment of great change and new choice disappointed you in ways you never imagined possible. What could I possibly have overlooked in the shaping of my life? you wondered.

You discovered frustration when what you wanted to have happen never did. You spent time and effort, you invested the very definition of yourself in it, and when you got to where you thought you wanted to go, realized that there was very little there. You began to understand the petty power of boredom. You found yourself lost in one dead end after another. You still cherished the high ideals that had brought you here but, in the end, found more of reality than the idealism you were seeking. Then you began to look beyond what you were doing to discover what you were meant to be.

Most surprising of all, everywhere you went you discovered that there were many more like you out there: war protesters who had given up and bought business suits; radical feminists who were once the harbingers of male/female separatism married and had a house full of children; poverty lawyers who left the storefront offices and bought into the firm; inner-city teachers who went back to a university, got a Ph.D., and stayed to do research.

But along with the disappointed ones, you found the liberated ones, as well. You discovered the other side of change, the side that spoke of fulfillment rather than discouragement. These were people who had grown into themselves, into the vision within them, to the point that change was the next straight step to their first and only dream. These people went from shop maintenance crew to shop foreman to small business owner, always doing more and better of what they always wanted to do and becoming more and more local philanthropist as they went. These people ventured beyond school teaching to positions on the school board. These people turned hobbies in woodworking into garage studios for furniture restoration and began an apprentice program for the next generation of young artists. You found people who went from cooking in fast-food restaurants to working as nutritionists in school cafeterias to see that children ate well enough to learn well, too.

All of them, all of them—like yourself—had tacked their way through life, catching one wind and then another, until the ship of life had finally come down even. Until they finally found themselves rather than the cardboard figures they had been trained to be. Rather than the shadow of someone else's dream that they—like you and I—had at one time tried so hard to be.

Then, one day, finally, you retired. It was then that you discovered that it wasn't the job that was either the problem or the solution to life. The problem was that you had struggled between passion and a paycheck. You thought a call had something to do with a job. You thought your purpose in life was to get a promotion in the land of interchangeable people. That way, you were sure, you could do good work for the company and for the world with it. Nor were you wrong. The integrity and commitment, the honesty and sense of justice you brought to your work gave substance to the corporate world's claims of probity. It was good work done well.

But now all that is over and the world looks very much as it did when first you began to take your place in its operation. Now what? What happens to the call of the heart now?

The problem is that the call that was never fully achieved in stages one and two has also never fully gone away. It has lain there in the depth of the soul, always beckoning, never completely achieved, never really forgotten or abandoned. Just put in abeyance, perhaps, or attended to, of course, but in fits and starts, casually, when everything else was finished. And yet the concern for the plight of abused children never really went away. The desire for peace in the world, for justice for minorities, for green energy and animal rights, for conservation or for participation in the political system, for the role of women in church and society, or for the time to read poetry and philosophy and great literature, for gardening, or for volunteering with the local search and rescue unit—or whatever—still make the heart beat a bit more strongly.

So has it all been a failure? On the contrary.

Now is the moment for the third phase of the call to personal destiny. Now, when all the routines of life have been met, now when all the daily responsibilities are over, the call to completion becomes the center of our lives.

All the parts of life meet in us here, at this point, and we are finally, fully, ready to give our best and our whole to the unanswered call that still lies unfinished within us. The secret to life is the willingness to grow into something that is beyond our present. Now, just when we think we are finished—without a scintilla of a reason to go on living full and significant lives—we find that the reason is in us still.

Carlos Castenada wrote, "All paths are the same: they lead nowhere. . . . In my own life I could say I have traversed long, long paths but I am not anywhere." This question has meaning now: "Does this path have a heart? If it does, the path is good. If it doesn't, it is of no use. Both paths lead nowhere: but one has a heart and the other doesn't. One makes for a joyful journey—as long as you follow it, you are one with it. The other will make you curse your life. One makes you strong; the other weakens you." Now is the time to make sure that the path we are on has heart, gives life, stirs our strength again.

For the first time at this stage of life we have the real freedom to do what we must. We have the experience to do it well. We have the responsibility to model for those who come after us what life is really meant to be about, what great things we are each called to do, what destiny awaits us outside the boundaries of our private little lives. We have the wisdom now to know what to do next and what not to do at all.

In the third stage of the call, we have enough of a self to give it away. It is not any longer what we accomplish that defines us. We have grown beyond that. Now we have only to witness to the world that life is about following the call, not about counting our accomplishments. The only real question worth anything at all in the pursuit of our life's purpose is Does this path have a heart?

It is this period of life that is the reason for which we have come. All the ambitious idealism of our beginnings has been lived through. We are not seeking simply to succeed now. All the disillusionment, all the unfinished striving of middle age has been negotiated. We have come, at long last, to understand that it is not excitement that the call has ever been about.

Instead, we know now that the call must indeed be

the sextant with which we choose our directions in life. A vocation to attend to the fullness of life within us is the heart we bring to our decision-making. It is not anything as mundane as work. It is far beyond the name on the door, the money in the bank, our position on the commercial ladder. It is the measure of our very selves, and it will be the eternal meaning of our lives.

Castenada is clear: the central question must always be—whatever our age or our place in life—Does this path have a heart? To do what is both meaningful to us and important to others is to have heart. To do more than merely survive at every age, more than breathing in and breathing out, is to have discovered the heart of life.

The undercurrent of the life well lived is the answer to the question Who or what would miss you if tomorrow you disappeared?

What is there to do now in this third phase of life? Oh, much. Very much indeed.

To know how to grow old is the master work of wisdom, and one of the most difficult chapters in the great art of living.

HENRI FREDERIC AMIEL

15.

IS EVERYTHING WE'D LIKE TO DO REALLY A CALL?

> *"I'm trying to decide whether I want to go into medicine or into business."*
>
> *"Well, what means most to you: what you'd like to be or what you hope to do with your life?"*
>
> *"Aren't they the same thing?"*
>
> *"Sometimes. If you're lucky. Or if you make them so."*

Somewhere along the line, the professions—medicine, law, teaching—took on the sense of a call, a vocation, a lifelong commitment to a special life task in the style of what religious vocations had always uniquely been seen to be.

Indeed, the professions are a lifestyle, not simply the kind of forty-hour-a-week job that most of us, whatever it is, are simply happy to have. The professions demand a kind of self-giving that most of us are either not able or not eager to do. The work hours are erratic. The public stress is constant. The need to be constantly available in one form or another can have an insidious effect on family life. Even the preparation required to qualify for such positions takes years to complete and years of debt to repay. Clearly, the determination to pursue lives like these demands great motivation, great persistence.

At the same time, it is more than possible to see them become vitiated—for money alone, or power alone, or prestige alone.

And therein lies the difference between a call and a profession, a certification and a commitment. Some people may like what they do because it's easy for them, because they do it well, because the pay is good, or because it gives them security and prestige, money and public influence. But other people do what they do for a reason beyond themselves, beyond the expression of talent, beyond the personal rewards, satisfying though these may be. They may certainly have a talent for their work. They may, in fact, do it very well. But to do it simply because they have a talent for it is not enough for them.

It is the desire to be the fullness of themselves and to serve others at the same time that drives them. It is the reason that some people give up selling stock or drilling for oil—where the commission is higher than the pay—in order to live out their lives in an African village drilling water wells or doing bed care for AIDS patients.

It is the difference between enthusiasm for the work and commitment to a life choice made as much with others in mind as for themselves.

I remember when I really began to understand those distinctions all too well. After over 100 years in what had recently become known as the inner city, insurance companies refused to the cover the original frame building that housed over 150 of us. One spark, they said, could burn down the entire monastery in minutes. The situation was dire: we couldn't afford to move and we couldn't afford to stay there either.

The decision was made to maintain our ministries in the inner city but, at the same time, to build on a piece of farmland outside the city. Our religious community had owned that piece of land since 1906, but we had never had the money to develop it.

The situation was a risk either way. It was a risk to have to build a new facility in a tentative economic climate, but it was, at the same time, a clear commitment to stay with the poor where we had always been.

So we broke ground and began the process of building a new monastery, which we trusted would pay for itself over the years.

But in the middle of the construction process, trade wars erupted everywhere. The price of steel tripled. Businesses closed. People were out of work. Bills came due. And this small women's religious community, accustomed to doing nothing but church-related works and living on small paychecks, which ran out at the end of the school year in May and did not start again till the end of September, could not afford to support themselves and go on paying building costs at the same time. It was the very definition of a dilemma: to stop construction and stay in the old monastery without insurance was not the answer. To go on without enough money to pay our bills was impossible.

We begged money from other communities, cut our own living expenses to the bone, and then in a last attempt at financial survival mounted a group of traveling choristers who sang all the way from local parishes to *The Ed Sullivan Show* on national TV. Then we made one final effort to balance our finances during the summer when there would be no parish income: we sent our young sisters out to clean the homes of wealthy families in the city till the funds began to flow again after we all went back to school in the fall.

Never had it been so clear to me that jobs and vocations, a call and a job, were not the same thing, as wonderful as it may be when the two can be one. Our vocation—to give our lives as witness to another way of life—never faltered. Our jobs had to change, however, in order to make that possible.

I learned, too, that commitment and enthusiasm are two concepts that are, unfortunately, often confused. Commitment is that quality of life that depends more on the ability to wait for something to come to fulfillment—through good days and through bad—than it does on being able to sustain an emotional extreme for it over a long period of time.

Enthusiasm, on the other hand, is excitement fed by satisfaction. The tangle of the two ideas, however, the propensity to mistake some kind of initial enthusiasm for commitment, is exactly what leads so many people to fall off in the middle of a project. When the work ceases to feel good, when praying for peace or working for women's rights or trying to save the whales or working with the poor gets nowhere, they lose interest in the project, call the ideals hopeless and the work useless and the efforts unsustainable.

When the marriage counseling fails to reinvigorate the level of excitement they remember as newlyweds, couples drift apart and go into second gear and begin to accommodate more, learn to put up with each other rather than set their hearts on making their love live again in new ways.

But it is precisely when the projects and the plans and the hopes dim—worse, when they fail and fizzle—that the sense of commitment really begins, really deepens.

When enthusiasm wanes and romantic love dies, and apathy—a debilitating loss of purpose and energy—sets in, that is the point at which we are asked to give as much as we get. That is the point when we decide whether we have a call to this particular life or not. That's when we decide whether we have found our real vocation—the reason for which we were really born—or not.

That's when what we thought was an adventure turns into a lifelong effort to become the fullness of our talents, the wholeness of our souls, a marker on the road to the totally human development of our small world. That is commitment: the sometimes long, hard, demanding dedication to something greater than our own gain or comfort or self-expression or security. It is watching what we started with enthusiasm turn into the demands of commitment that can tempt us to despair. Yet, at the center of us, we know that the God who created us with this gift, this call, this talent will surely sustain us in the doing of it. As if the God whose voice we follow will ever abandon the good. As if waiting for God's good time was a waste of our time. As if God's love will ever fail us in the end.

A vocation, a call to be wholehearted co-creators of life, is wreathed in blinding light in an ancient American Indian story—far more clearly than in any recruitment poster or vocation talk:

> "Tell me the weight of a snowflake," a coal mouse asked a wild dove.
>
> "Nothing more than nothing," the dove answered.
>
> "In that case I must tell you a marvel-

ous story," the coal mouse said. "I sat on a fir branch close to the trunk when it began to snow. Not heavily, not in a raging blizzard. No, just like in a dream, without any violence at all. Since I didn't have anything better to do, I counted the snowflakes settling on the twigs and needles of my branch. Their number was exactly 3,471,952. When the next snowflake dropped onto the branch—nothing more than nothing—as you say—the branch broke off." Having said that, the coal mouse ran away.

The dove, since Noah's time an authority on peace, thought about the story for a while. Finally, she said to herself, "Perhaps there is only one person's voice lacking for peace to come to the world."

Commitment is that quality of human nature that tells us not to count days or months or years, struggle or effort or rejection, but simply to go on until the work we have come to do is done, whether the need is finally, completely, finished or not. That can be finished by those who come after us. What is imperative to the honoring of a call, to the meaning of a vocation, is that we give our own life to the doing of it.

When we feel most discouraged, most fatigued, most alone is precisely the time we must not quit. It is precisely then that the call we have—that blend of passion and purpose—speaks most deeply to the deepest core of us.

It is with many enterprises as with striking fire; we do not meet with success except by reiterated efforts, and often at the instant when we despaired of success.

FRANÇOISE DE MAINTENON

16.

HOW DO I KNOW IF I HAVE A CALL?

*"I think there's more to me than the job
I'm in, but I don't know how to find out what
it is."*

*"Well, what do you care enough about to
spend your life on?"*

The call came months after the earthquake in Haiti, after the story had cooled on television, after most people had long ago moved on in life. I remember it with startling accuracy: "I just couldn't get the picture of those Haitian children out of my mind," the woman's voice on the other end of the phone said. "They looked so fragile, so wounded, so vulnerable, so beautiful." There was a pause on the line. "I just knew that I had to do something about it—but it seemed that I couldn't do anything at all."

Not too long ago, when a person said that they were trying to discern whether or not they had a call in life, they were talking about considering the possibility of doing something religious in life—like becoming a minister or a rabbi or a priest. Now it's not that easy anymore. Call, in our age, has become a bit of everything—and, at the same time, nothing that specific. The concept of being called to something, set apart from the rest of the world, made particular, marked in a special way, by the divine—is long gone.

In its place, the concept of discovering our call in life has become more confusing, more difficult to identify than any single work. To feel a "call" now is not about having a particular job or role in life. It's not about anything simply ecclesiastical or credal. No, now it has become far more important than that.

Call, we have come to understand, is an amorphous response to an undetermined internal search for a meaningful life, a shapeless longing to do something of value on the great journey from time to eternity. The problem for our time, in other words, is not the lack of human commitment. On the contrary. In this world of expanding outreach and global possibilities, people seek something worth committing their lives to doing. The problem lies, rather, in thinking that a call is something outside ourselves, rather than realizing that a call is actually the longing inside ourselves to become fully human, and waiting to be transformed into flesh and blood. Ours.

The short answer, then, to the question of whether or not average people—people like us—have a call is a clear one: everybody has a call to something. Some call it "the priesthood of believers." Some call it "the will of God for us." Some call it co-creation. But they all mean the same thing. We have each been born with particular gifts of mind and soul, of body and brain, of personality and skill that we are meant to use for the greater good. There is no such thing as not having a call.

After all, we all come into this world equipped to do something of value, to become someone who will benefit the human race, to do something that brings creation closer to fulfillment. Anything else is to be less than we are meant to be, to do less than we can do.

We are not born to be a biological overrun. We come into this world as a unique gift and grace to others, called to life itself and meant to be life-giving to someone else. Life is simply the process of becoming whatever that is. The task, then, is to determine how I can do that best.

So the question is not How do I know if I have a call? The only real question is How do I know what that call is?

The depth of the human struggle that underlies that question is enough to shake the human soul. It separates the adolescent from the adult, the person who has a job from the person who has a life, the giver from the taker, the spiritual seeker who believes that the universe has a purpose from the materialist who believes that the planet was made for our personal exploitation and life for our particular satisfaction. Or, worse, that there is no use to life at all and no meaning to our own.

Clearly there is something we are meant to be, if for no other reason than that we are the particular person we are: the one with the smile, with the sensitivity, with the skill, with the personality, with the sense of purpose and commitment and passion to do well this particular thing that the rest of the world needs at this particular time.

And yet, at the same time, there are so many options now, at least theoretically, that the very notion of a conscious and spiritual choice has, in our time, become a relatively superficial one. Until now. Until the global economic reality made short shrift of the candy-store mentality toward life that preceded it. "I've decided to quit my job at the restaurant," the young man told me. "Why?" I asked him. "I thought you liked it there." He countered quickly, "Well, I thought I did but now they want me to do evenings three nights a week and I don't like that." I waited for what he did want to do instead. "So," he went on, "I think I'll just travel for a while and see what's out there."

It isn't that the laissez-faire lifestyle went out with the Bohemians, but as an essential part of the search for meaning in life it has certainly lost its cachet.

The notion of unending possibilities, of endless options, of the guarantee of years of shopping around to find something that suits our schedule as well as our interests ends somewhere along the line—for whatever reasons, personal or financial. And with it go dreams of faraway places and exotic fantasies. We know now that there are more serious reasons on which to spend a life. Now the needs of the human race live in our hometowns and in global villages everywhere. In Technicolor. Life has become a community endeavor again. None of us can afford to think of ourselves as self-sufficient, not even millionaires with overextended mortgages nor middle-class families with college fees to face. Nor can any of us afford to assume that we can be complacently dependent on the rest of the human race to sustain us in a world where sustenance is now a global concern.

And yet the problem is not really an economic one at all. The problem is a spiritual one. Cultures without a strong sense of moral obligation or spiritual depth breed populations with an even weaker sense of social obligation or spiritual purpose.

Everything in such a society is geared to my getting ahead, to living my life, to succeeding according to standards that add nothing to the soul and little even to the rest of life—the expensive car, for instance, the social invitation list, perhaps, the appearance of luxury that comes with those deeply in debt. It is a plastic world that lives on credit cards and totally out of touch with the true self. It is a world that borrows someone else's definition of purpose or happiness and seldom, if ever, examines its own. Until, mired in the plastic goals of a plastic world, we find ourselves too soulless to claim our own.

It is difficult in such a climate to recognize that I am important, not because I am important to me—in the narcissistic sense of the word—but because I am important to you, to the rest of the family and the city and the world around me.

It is difficult in such a world to develop a sense of purpose beyond myself. It is almost impossible to feel passion for the needs of others when I am consumed by what I have learned to want rather than what the world needs.

It is those with a passion for life—for all life—and for the life they have to give to it who feel the call stir within them at the sight of another's need. Then, when the talent within them stirs in response to it, the call comes to life.

About the telephone call that started this chapter: The woman who made that phone call was employed as a stagehand on Broadway. One day, working backstage on props and sets, she realized that the metal struts that support the sets and backdrops of the great shows mounted there are routinely discarded after every production. Then everything became clear: she managed to procure those metal strips and used them to design, build, and erect geodesic domes in Haiti to house the orphans still without shelter in the mud of that ravaged land. In between segments of the project, she returned to her job in New York City.

She had found her call and she followed it. Or to put it another way, the television films of wide-eyed, shocked, lonely, and abandoned children broke through the normal protections of her normal life to engage all the passion in her soul. The purpose, the goal, the expression of it followed easily.

Passion answers the question What moves my heart? Purpose answers the question What can I do about it? That's what call is about: it is the passion that stirs the heart and the sense of purpose it takes to move a life beyond the dailiness of life as usual, beyond routine to involvement.

No, a call is not a job. It is far more than that. It is the burning desire to do something of meaning in the world. Even corporations are now discovering the notion of shared value, the idea that corporations are for more than making profit for themselves. They must also have, they now say, a social purpose, a corporate mission. "When you understand the impact you can have," Bill Green, chairman of Accenture, said to corporate executives, "then you are on a mission, then this becomes spiritual, it becomes part of the DNA of the company."

It is a matter of making life and work one. But to do that, corporations have begun to say, they must give more than checks to charity. Instead, they must begin to give to the world communal gifts that make their presence among us more than simply local industries but a call and obligation to have a profound effect on many of the most important social issues of our time. Food companies, for instance, can enable small farmers to get the education that improves farming. Power producers can pursue alternative forms of energy. Large retailers can reduce the amount of packaging they use and so reduce their carbon footprint.

Clearly, for those for whom the job and the call are one, life is whole. For those with a job that enables a response to the call, their lives are whole. For those with a call so strong, so clear, that their job sustains them but their call energizes them, their lives, too, are whole and happy. We are all called, in some form and fashion, to give ourselves away so that tomorrow can be better than yesterday for many. We are all called to be reckless, intrepid, conscious philanthropists of the world to come.

The foolish seek happiness in the distance; the wise grow it under their feet.
JAMES OPPENHEIM

17

HOW DO I KNOW I'M DOING WHAT I'M MEANT TO DO?

> *"I just heard that you got laid off. I'm so sorry."*
>
> *"Oh, please, don't be. I am finally able to do what I've always wanted to do. I've never in my life been happier than I am right now."*

Success is a great American virtue. Headlines declare it everywhere. Society at large rewards success with reckless extravagance: with affection, with attention, with compensation, with public positions. Who wouldn't seek it?

But what this culture calls success, I think has really very little to do with lasting success at all. The newspapers are as full of stories that confirm the collapse of success as they are of the full-page, four-color pictures that herald it. Those who have achieved the wealth or notoriety, fame or public office, achievement or power that brought them all the attention in the first place are its targets as well. The media, they soon learn, dote just as much on the social carcasses of celebrities whose lives seem to have unraveled under the strain of the very kinds of success they sought. They detail the marriages that break down, the bodies that wilt from the parties, the drugs, and the drink that the fast life has to offer, until eventually the very talents that brought the rich and the famous to the pinnacles of fame and wealth and public attention crush them under the weight of bearing them.

So did they succeed or not?

Wisdom figures of every age have defined success very differently than our culture does: "The first and best victory," Plato said, "is the ability to conquer self." And the Native Americans taught, "The great are those who attempt the difficult things which lesser people avoid."

The question is then how do we tell the difference between being successful according to someone else's terms and doing with "your one wild and precious life," as the poet Mary Oliver said of it, the best of which we are capable, the finest we can, regardless of anyone else's determinations for us? How can we be happy even if we never know the kind of success of which this era's headlines are made?

Can anyone really know whether they're doing what they are supposed to be doing or not? What does it mean, in fact, to ask whether or not I am doing what I am meant to do or was born to do?

I smiled a bit as I began to write this chapter. The fact is that I know the difference between what it means to do what you were born to do and doing something else, equally good, perhaps, but not nearly as right for you. After all, I have been there. I spent years doing what was surely a very good thing, doing what people told me was important and that I did well. But, secretly, privately, I always knew that there was more, more than teaching, that was really the fullness of me. Until that part of life started, I could feel the vacuum within me just waiting to be filled. But with what?

In that sense of being suspended over life lies the secret of recognizing a call.

The sense of meaning in our lives which we spend so many years looking for, seeking to have confirmed, wanting to achieve is actually within us all the while. It does not come from outside of us at all. In fact, we are born equipped for it. If there is such a thing as the law of attraction it is certainly here in this inner journey to determine where we are to be in life and what we are to do. The truth is that, as if there were a magnet within us, we tend constantly toward the fulfillment of the self.

In seeking to find whatever it is to which we are called in life, we need to understand that we are meant to become what we already are in the undercurrent of the self. We are not meant to become something different, something less than what we can be. We are meant to follow the call that is already an embryo in us to the completion of ourselves. We live our lives in search of this rest of us. Our internal compass is set always in the direction of the rest of us, not something unlike us or impossible for us or inimical to us. In fact, it is just those very things that stand to destroy us.

To discover our call then requires that we come to recognize seven dimensions of an authentic call, the seven dimensions of life in us seeking to be fully engaged in the enterprise of being alive in both body and soul.

First, to find what we know to be our call in life, we must be looking for something that fits our skills, not something that fits someone else's ideas of what they would like to see us do. My mother's older sisters had all taken violin lessons. None of them liked music; none of them really practiced; none of them took to the instrument, and all of them stopped taking music lessons early on. When my mother came along, she wanted to learn to play the piano instead. The answer was a take-it-or-leave-it deal: if she really wanted music lessons, they told her, it had to be on the violin. Clearly, the family wasn't going to waste any more money on unused instruments. And just as clearly, my mother had no intention of wasting her time on an instrument in which she had no interest. Who won the argument? It all depends on how you look at it. One outcome, however, emerges: no wonder it can take so many years for some people to identify what it is in them that strains to find expression and what they must do to find the means to do so. When life itself is an obstacle to the claiming of the true self, the whole process of becoming fully alive can be stifled.

Second, a real call in life is for something that goes beyond either interest or ability. A real call strikes white hot passion in a person. I know a young woman who came from a highly commercial and public family. They were philanthropists, financiers, corporate professionals, entrepreneurs, business types. Maggie, on the other hand, loved horses. She didn't want to go to college; she wanted to be a horsewoman. All she felt called to do in life was to train horses and run a riding school. It was hardly the kind of thing the family could have either predicted or planned. In the end, however, Maggie spun her love for horses into the creation of one of the first riding schools in the country for emotionally disturbed children. She tells the story with a light in her eyes that nothing else she talks about begins to ignite.

Third, my call is what drives me beyond both talent and passion to a sense of purpose. I know with a kind of certainty clearer than anything else in my life that there is not only something I would like to do but something I intend to do. Something I must do. The effects of a great sense of purpose appear in every edition of the daily paper. It is, for instance, the story about musicians around the country coming together to use their talents to feed the hungry in Africa. It is the picture of an eye doctor setting up cataract clinics in Latin America, alone and single-handed. It is my doing what I do best to make the world conscious that life must be better, happier, more just for someone else.

Fourth, my call presents itself as a thorn in my heart at the sight of another's pain. It stops life in its tracks. Or it comes as a happy leap of the soul to another whole level of insight whenever I get anywhere near what holds me enthralled. It may come as a lingering image of someone or something I cannot forget. Whatever its form, my life falls captive to a picture or a feeling that will not go away, that haunts my steps and focuses my life like a laser beam. I may work at Walmart, but I spend all my free time rescuing stray animals or volunteering on environmental projects or teaching English to immigrants at night or studying the chemistry of glazes in order to propel the art world one more step toward staggering beauty. This great gaping awareness of what is missing in the world stirs a gift in me that makes all the anonymous figures I touch with it real, personal, part of my life. This is not work I am doing. This is life, up close and personal. Theirs as well as mine.

Fifth, when I am following my call, I lose all sense of time. I am, as athletes say, "in the zone." This thing I am doing is the whole universe of my life. It is not drudgery. It is not disgusting. It is everything life is about for me—all wrapped into one clear moment of life. And I am one great living desire to connect to it, somehow. It is small starving dogs in a puppy mill that leads me to become intent on passing legislation to protect animals everywhere. It is my need to do one more oil painting to enhance an otherwise phony world. It is the energy problem of the globe for which I have a small but plausible plan for solving. It may be the subject of oppression, injustice, domination, and destruction that I refuse to allow the world to forget in my presence.

Sixth, when I discover my call in life, when I know in my heart where I am supposed to be and what I am supposed to do, I find that I am as much expanded by whatever it is that I'm doing as it is by me. I learn things I never expected from this giving of the self. I learn about myself and am humbled by it. I learn about life and am astounded by it. I learn about success and discover that life's only real success requires that I end life still learning, still giving, still growing, still reaching for the unreachable dream of my heart.

Seventh, to become what I am born to do, what I am uniquely capable of doing is, in the end, good for the soul as well as for the work. It changes me. I find out that happiness is a lot less and a lot more than I ever expected. I may come to know what Aristotle really meant when he said that life was about living well and doing good. It is about doing something worth doing and doing it to my utmost degree; it is about living to the highest boundaries of my humanity and making life more human around me. That sense of satisfaction is its reward. That sense of completeness is happiness. Then, as we are fond of saying, when we look back, we will know that it has all been right.

Three grand essentials to happiness in this life are something to do, something to love, and something to hope for.

JOSEPH ADDISON

WHAT DOES A SENSE OF CALL HAVE TO DO WITH THE SPIRITUAL LIFE?

"Some people talk about having a call in life. I'd just be happy if I had a good job."
"Are you talking about being happy or being secure?"

⌒

For the first time in history, in 2009 two satellites in earth's orbit crashed into each other and were destroyed. More than that, the same source reports that there are now millions of orbital ruins that make up what we call space junk. Most important of all, they tell us, these basically infinitesimally small objects traveling at speeds of 17,500 mph are capable of causing major damage to orbiting craft. Even a small speck of paint, we're told, can do serious damage to orbiting craft. Who is there who could possibly fail to imagine the growing effect of this kind of situation on eons to come?

Indeed, the application of such an image to the

human psyche, to life, to our own sense of self-fulfillment, in the here and now, is a compelling one.

A veritable cauldron of memories, the human mind, like outer space, preserves and catalogues everything that has ever happened to it—some of it positive, some of it not. Exactly what kind of effect each of these small, single experiences can have on us, no one is sure. But the metaphor of the consequence of unresolved bits of life on the rest of life is simply too impacting to ignore. To simply float through life like a piece of human equipment without passion, without purpose, is to barter the very essence of life, both psychological and spiritual. In failing to become the entirety of what we are meant to be, we become a kind of social hazard to others as well as to ourselves. But there are other possibilities.

"Life is a pure flame," Thomas Browne wrote, "and we live by an invisible sun within us." It is this invisible sun, this light within, this call to something worthwhile in life that is meant to dispel life's darkness. It gives us our reason to be. And it is this call to the fullness of ourselves that drives us on, that becomes our internal measure of worth and, in the end, it is, as well, the judge of our quality of happiness.

Life is not about having a job. Life is about responding to the great human call to make life more than a series of aimless occupations. A call is a sacred reason to be alive.

The spiritual value of discovering the star by which

we are steering the entire rest of our lives shapes us both internally and publically. It affects the way we feel about ourselves, it determines how we relate to others, it defines our place in the world, and it provides a sense of purpose to life. When those things are defined, the emptiness goes, the rootlessness goes, the capriciousness of life that eats away at the heart of us disappears. Days may be difficult after that, yes, but they at least have a sense of meaning. We are no longer simply spinning around in the space called our lives, fearful of the future, dissatisfied with the present. We are now someone going someplace for a reason larger than ourselves and feeling more humanly significant than simply self-important.

Nothing disquiets the soul more than a feeling of being unfinished, adrift, and rudderless at the same time. There is something more we're meant to do in life, we're sure, but no way, apparently, to dispel the aura of aimlessness in which we have begun to live. I go to work every morning but no amount of money could really make me like it, feel good about being there, able to convince myself that being there is where I'm meant to be.

There is a cosmic sense of frustration about knowing myself to be on the way to somewhere—but in the dark. I do my best at everything I do, however mundane, however humble. I know that cooking hamburgers in a short-order place is a decent thing to do in life. But I can't believe that is all I'm meant to do in life. There must be more. There simply must be more I'm supposed to be doing than making hamburgers for people who can pay for them.

I avoid class reunions because everybody else there talks big plans about big things, but nothing big has ever happened to me. Nor have I begun yet to realize that there is a distinction between going to work and pursuing my call. So I go through life disappointed with the job but unable to realize that the call, for me, may be far and wide away from any paid occupation anywhere.

I have yet to understand that my call may start after work ends every day. My call may be to organize games for street children, or read to blind people, or picket political offices, or write to prisoners, or make casseroles for the old woman next door, or learn another language in order to help refugees adapt to the small white town in which I live.

The point is clear: my sense of worth and purpose in life is tied up with the quality of life I provide for others, for the planet, for the human race. Solving equations all day long, or encoding a computer all day long can also be boring, can also seem worthless, unless I'm doing these things in order to be some small part in curing an insidious disease or finding a formula that reduces the world's dependence on fossil fuels.

It may be something as simple as producing materials that ennoble the human mind rather than pander to it, selling and creating things that enhance life rather than destroy it. And, yes, making hamburgers for those who can pay for them can also be a call, provided that working in this place is what enables me to care consciously for someone else in some other way.

In the end, it is passion and purpose—passion and purpose—that are of the essence of a vocation, a call to do something that makes me a conscious co-creator of the world.

An old medieval story may make the point best. A traveler came across three stonecutters. "What are you doing?" the traveler asked the first man.

"I am making a living," the man said.

"And what are you doing?" the traveler asked the second man.

And that man said, "I am practicing to become the best stonecutter in Europe."

Then the man asked the third laborer. And the third man answered, "I am building a cathedral."

In my commitment to my vocation, whatever it may be—helping cripples to walk and people to die dignified deaths and children to learn and the world to grow seeds and nations to live in peace—I myself become a holy person, a mystic whose God is alive and present and waiting for us to do what must be done to make creation itself a holy place.

A call demands endurance and persistence, commitment and stability. To be a real call it must be something worth giving my time, my resources, myself to doing. It has nothing to do with success as measured in the numbers of people served or the numbers of units produced or the number of events attended. It has everything to do with trying. As the Sufi say, "If you are expecting to find an answer to your problem, you have simply not asked a big enough question." It is out of an awareness of our role on earth that we find our place on earth.

The point is clear: my sense of worth and purpose in life is tied up with the quality of life I develop in myself in order to provide the same for others, for the planet, for the human race. It is then, surely, when we are most concerned with life as God meant it to be, that we come closest to godlike ourselves.

If there is a sin against life, it lies perhaps less in despairing of it than in hoping for another and evading the implacable grandeur of the one we have.

ALBERT CAMUS

19.

SHOULD I TRY VARIOUS THINGS BEFORE DECIDING WHAT TO DO?

*"Do you know yet what you want to do
with your life?"*
*"Not really. Maybe horticulture; maybe
psychotherapy."*

I came from a normal kind of Catholic family for that
era and place: the aunts went to church; the uncles
didn't. But we all agreed that the church was a good
thing and important to us, culturally as well as spiritually. To be part of a parish, to go to a Catholic school,
to be a member maybe of one of those ubiquitous private ethnic clubs as much defined by religion as they
were by nationality went with the territory. It was all
simply part of being card-carrying Catholics. Until.

Until the word went through the family under-
ground that I had decided to go to a monastery. Then
family I hadn't seen for years began to show up to talk
to me. The uncles were the clearest of all. Church

people were good people, they said. Where would we be without them, in fact? But I, they said, simply did not have the personality for a monastery. I was too active, too fun-loving, too outgoing. I needed to cancel those plans and see the world before I did anything like that. Going to a monastery was definitely not for me.

And, if truth were known, I had some important misgivings about it myself. I was an only child. To leave my mother in a position where she could easily be without family, without care and support in the future was a real possibility. But, in addition to this consideration, there was another one. I had discovered early in high school that I was a writer and I wanted to be a writer as much as I wanted to be a nun. No nuns I knew were writers. Nor were many women anywhere.

So how does something like this get decided? Do we take the first thing available and hope that it all comes out right? Or do we ourselves do nothing—and hope that things come out all right? Do we decide—or does God, the default explanation for being catapulted into something rather than making a decision ourselves. Do we choose something in contrast to something else or should we simply wait till whatever it might be that is really right for us simply comes along and chooses us?

The most important answer to any question is not the answer; it is the reason that underlies the answer that counts. Or to put it another way, the answer to whether or not we should try things in life while we're trying to decide what it is that really engages us, both heart and soul, must surely be definitely yes. But at the same time, it is also definitely no. Life is not a merry-go-round of exercises in interest, all of them neutral.

What is a call then? It is life lived in recognition of what we're able to do, what we want to do, and what needs to be done for some good purpose.

If one of the signs of a genuine call is that it is built right into our very being, or if, as the ancients put it, God never asks anything of us that we are not able to deliver, then what we know about ourselves is as essential to the process of following our call as what we think would be good or exciting or prestigious. I may want to work at the United Nations, but if I have no facility for languages, all the study in the world may not fit me for it. In which case, that is more than likely not what I am being called to do in life. At least not as an interpreter.

The second problem may be that in this culture we are inclined to confuse an occupation, a career, with the call to a wholeness of the self. Or we confuse a call to personal development with a call to spiritual development. We confuse the call to the full development of ourselves with the pursuit of full physical or economic development. We confuse our commitment to the self with a call to be about something bigger than ourselves, our egos, our badges of fleeting and ephemeral success. A call is about something a great deal more critical than any of those. It is about finding what it is that grows our souls rather than simply our bodies or our social life. The microscopic attention to the nurturance of the ego is no substitute for the development of the spiritual self.

We were not born to make money or accumulate things or get power—all of which are good but none of which is enough to assure that life as we live it will really be enriching, of importance to someone other than simply ourselves. Discovering what our call is and doing it is the mark of the truly fulfilled and happy life.

There is a spot in the human soul that is empty of the self and meant to be filled with the concerns and needs of others. To leave life without having done that is to have lived into the epitome of emptiness. When we get more money than we can spend, when we have more than enough money for our own needs, what else can we get ourselves that will really change life for us? Once we have exhausted the self in its own interests, what else is there for us in life beyond the geography of our own smallness?

When we're done buying all the gadgets, taking all the trips, hosting all the dinners, going to all the parties that life has to offer, we will be satiated, of course, but we will not necessarily be better human beings than we were before. We will simply be glutted human beings, too engorged with all the things life has to offer to be moved beyond any of them to all the joy of being alive. Then when we have exhausted our senses it will be our souls that cry out for attention, for the joy of being alive. Finding our call, determining what it is that is meant to be our gift to creation, and then giving our lives to it, is as much about becoming the height and breadth and depth of our own humanity as it is about enabling the humanity of others. We are, indeed, "our brother's keepers," as the scriptures say. To leave out that part of our humanity is to dwarf our own.

Raw ability, deep interests, and personal commitment are the stuff it takes to find and shape and live into our call to both become something worth becoming and to give something worth giving to the rest of the world. To be a fully developed human being requires that we attend to the tender nourishment of the human soul beyond its physical appetites to the point of "virtuous action" and the spiritual depth that flows from it.

I didn't go out to see the world, as my uncles suggested. I insisted on following the haunting possibility within me that the pursuit of the spiritual life was itself an impactingly public and searingly personal call at the same time. I determined that I would stay with it till its ability to stretch me and challenge me might end. It is years later and I am still doing that. It's a small and hidden gift but it is the only one I have to give.

And, oh yes, along the way I also became the gift I had given up to do it. I began to write about spiritual issues and discovered that they were my central interest and exactly what other people were grappling with as well. It's a small contribution, perhaps, but it is the one that gathered into one place what I knew to be my natural abilities, my endless interest, a lifetime worth of spiritual commitment and my own small way of trying to contribute to the spiritual development of the world around me in a time of great change and even greater spiritual questions.

A useless life is an early death.

GOETHE

20.

IS IT POSSIBLE TO HAVE MORE THAN ONE CALL?

"I've been doing this for over twenty years. It must be time for a change."

"Don't you think it's pretty late in life just to pick up and take off?"

"Actually, all I know for sure is that life's not over till it's over."

Newspapers are full of stories about people whose lives change, it seems, in midair. Sometimes the reversals are drastic. More often they seem more subtle than startling. But whatever the nature of the change, it is always determinative. Even in your life and mine. Hurricane Carter, for instance, was a young man whose rise out of a New Jersey ghetto to the level of contender for the 1964 title of middleweight champion of the world was meteoric. Three years later he was convicted of murder and sentenced to three life terms in prison for a crime he did not commit. It was twenty-one years later before that sentence was finally overturned.

He once "boxed to make a living," he says, but since his release from prison he has been fighting for the release of others whose cases are tenuous but ignored, because "innocent people in prison rarely have anyone in their corner."

Carter was a fighter who used his physical abilities to overcome the racism of his time. Now he uses his moral and spiritual gifts to fight for the rights of others.

Did Carter have one call or two? Or was Carter's one great life-changing call simply a result of doing differently what he had been doing in the first place? Struggling for just recognition first for himself and then, later, for others whose place in life left them essentially invisible and powerless. So what difference does it make just because he found himself and his place in life late and slowly? The point is that life is about living into the one great moment of insight, awareness, realization that changes us so that we can do what we are meant to do to change it for others, as well.

For numbers of alcoholics, it is the very process of defeating alcoholism that makes them valued mainstays for others who are also struggling to do the same.

Only after years of thinking that life is all about making money do many philanthropists come to realize that a sense of life's real fulfillment lies in giving it away.

So what is it saying to us about what it means to

give our lives to the service of a call rather than simply to the search for security? Surely it's this: life is a process; not a recipe. Plutarch said of it over two thousand years ago, "Abstruse questions must have abstruse answers." So much of life is incomprehensible; it is no wonder that our answers to it are also abstruse and our paths to them so often twisted. Who of us can explain the circuitous meanderings of our own lives otherwise? How exactly did I get to this keyboard in this place, for instance? Only, I know now, through the labyrinth of time that took me down one dead end, one more apparently useless turn after another, till I find myself here, where I least expected I would ever finally arrive. Yet I am certainly where I am meant to be. But I didn't know that—at least I wasn't sure of it—for years.

Life is not a straight line, no matter how hard we work to make it so, no matter how certain we are that it must be. Life, it seems, is a cosmic game of dice: in today's society we are born in one town, raised in another, go to school in a third, settle down in a fourth, and retire in a fifth. Those aren't plans; those are happenstances, the pulp out of which we are to mold a life and develop a passion and find a purpose and leave a legacy to the next generation to come. As Ralph Waldo Emerson said, "Life is a succession of lessons which must be lived to be understood. We are meant to shape our souls out of the leavings of it and, rich or poor, female or male, leave this world less a statistic and more an icon to light the way for those who are to follow us. Anything else is not a life at all; it is at best an existence."

Nor, then, is a call an end point of life. On the contrary, it is only the beginning. My call is the point at which I begin to work out in myself what I am really meant to do in life that justifies my existence, that gives me the right to have been born.

For years, life is all about ourselves. It is those years that are the adolescence of the spiritual life. We spend them thinking that what we are meant to do is about us. It can take years before we find out that life is at least as much about what we are meant to do for others. We spend those early years looking for God's plan for us. But the black box theology of life—the notion that somewhere out there lies a schema for our lives that we are to discover before it's too late to get it right—quickly disappoints.

That kind of thinking takes us into great philosophical and theological quagmires of stifling proportions. If we think about it long enough we find ourselves face-to-face with the question of evil: how can a good God allow bad things to happen to us? Or we begin to wonder about the question of free will: if God knows everything before it happens, how can we say that there is any such thing as free will? Or if God has a plan for us, what is the use of our taking years to discover or develop it? Only when we stop thinking of God as playing a game with us to see if we can get the very question of what to do with our lives right, do we begin to realize the call is a partnership. God gives us our gifts; we are meant to discover how to best use them for the sake of the world, both now and to come. God companions us on the way and receives our effort at the end. God beckons us forward when we would fail ourselves and quit.

We struggle to discover what God has decided we are supposed to do in life until we finally stumble into it and realize that, in fact, we were endowed with it from the beginning. In which case, of course, our one task was to discover how to know what it was and then to do it.

So we move from here to there, from this to that as we go, driven by fame or fortune, good luck or good fun, prestige or profit until we have bankrupted all of them and found ourselves yet unfulfilled. Then one day, if we take the time to think it all through, we become spiritual adults and stop blaming God. Or, to put it another way, if God has plotted a "plan" for us, what kind of a God is it that would hide it from us, play a kind of divine hide-and-seek with it, and leave us wanting to do what we're meant to do in life without the vaguest notion of how to tell what that is?

No, a call is neither a divine contest of wits nor a divine message. A call is what we have been given for the sake of both fullness of life and divine service. It is the compilation of our natural abilities and interests, our fiercest commitments and passions, which then become the purpose of our lives. It is that in me which makes the world a better place to be and shapes the entirety of myself as well. Finding that amalgam of gifts and circumstances in life can conceivably take years and demand multiple attempts in the process, all of them side roads to the destination of the self. But in the end, it is ourselves that we will find there.

Prison, Hurricane Carter wrote, is what helped him realize that his destiny could lie in lacing up his gloves to fight for others.

Is there more than one call? Probably not, though there are certainly variations of it along the way embedded in everything we do. But without a doubt, each of the byways on the road is a small step on the way to it. As Emerson taught, life is a "progress," a passage through time, "not a station," never a stopping place. It is a progression of events that lead to insight, to self-knowledge, to the direction of the home within. One experience at a time, we begin to understand who we really are and what happiness really is for us. Then, what the poet Emerson wrote becomes glaringly clear: life, he said, "is a succession of lessons which must be lived to be understood."

Life is a quarry, out of which we are to mold and chisel and complete a character.

GOETHE

21.

IS IT EVER TOO LATE
TO START OVER?

"You're still at the store! I thought you were going to be a doctor?"
"I've always wanted to but couldn't. Now it's way too late for that."

Terry Fator is a young man most people had never heard of when he was the lead singer for a small band in Texas and making money on the side doing ventriloquism acts at country fairs. Everything about the situation was wrong: First, ventriloquism had long since died out as a public art in the United States. Second, most people think of ventriloquism as a children's show. Third, as Fator put it, when he did manage to get a place at a local fair, the organizers scheduled his appearance during the hottest part of the day and put him "on a back stage next to the wheelie ride where the act couldn't even be heard over the noise."

In the meantime, the band, what he considered his

real job, languished in local invisibility. They played just well enough to stay in business but were treading water, mired in the unending unknown. It was a living but for Fator it was not a life. So one night he put his two loves—singing and ventriloquism— together. He added the ventriloquist characters to his solos and watched the people in the bar come to life. It was that night, over thirty years after he had started doing ventriloquism as a boy, that his future began. The audience exploded in delight. Fator auditioned for *America's Got Talent* and went from there to playing long-standing engagements in Las Vegas.

He became what he always wanted to be: a ventriloquist who was a singer.

It wasn't his job that took him there; it was doing what he did best, what he loved doing and which, long years later, in the end, brought him to where he had always known he should be, using a little-known art to bring a few moments of innocent entertainment to a world in depression and stumbling through dire straits.

Question: Did he fail in life or did he succeed? Answer: That depends as much on how we look at it as how he looks at it.

It all depends on what we ourselves value—fast money or human happiness. Surely this man could have made more money a lot sooner in a bank or in business, in development or law—even doing comedy skits that bordered on the bawdy and the banal. But he wasn't looking for a quick fix or big money. What he wanted was to bring the talents within him to the point of ultimate development, to the paramount in comedic art, like the jesters of centuries before him. It took thirty years for Fator to become what he set out to be, most of them spent hidden in county fairs, all of them undervalued for either their worth or their artistry.

And, as a result, he becomes a template for our own lives.

The fact is that life is lived in stages, and each stage has its meaning and its purpose. One builds on the other; one prepares for the other; each one is different from the other. And none of them can be rushed. Only in an age of toasters and television sets, of digital communication and social networking have we learned to expect instant results in anything. As a consequence, the pace of life has quickened but the pace of learning and human ripening has not.

Images of instant success fade from the screen as quickly as they appeared, and the memories of them are very few and very far between. If truth were known, we all grow into the breadth of ourselves one period at a time, none of them complete, none of them final until life is final.

Clearly, Emerson was right. Life really is "a succession of lessons which must be lived to be understood." To attempt to leap over the learning of any of them simply means that they will need to be learned at another time if we are ever to be whole. We mature at our own pace and what is building in us now will, if we will only allow it, someday, somehow, emerge in us and cry out for expression.

Then, at that point, we ourselves must decide whether we will give light and life to those ripening parts of us or not.

It's a risk, of course, to recognize the slow birth in us of elements so long suppressed that they are no longer welcomed, not only by others but even by ourselves. It's an even greater risk to embrace it. "At your age" becomes the chant of inhibition, and "Now it's too late for that" becomes the anthem of despair. Internal constraints set in and we surrender to the loss of what we never insisted must be developed in us. So a part of us shrivels inside of us and another whole part of us lies stillborn one more time.

But at the same time, to accept the risk of coming late to the self is to accept the heady ecstasy of becoming the whole gamut of the self. I remember watching my father rock back and forth on the edge of the living room couch, old mandolin on his knee, eyes closed, with just enough beer in him to ignore the chants and anthems and become again what as a boy he had always dreamed about being.

I remember the sadness in a young man's eyes as he told me, MBA in hand, that he had really always wanted to be a history professor but his father simply wouldn't hear of it. In his house, he explained to me, you were sent to college so you could make good

money, not to live in the past. His eyes, I noticed, sad-
dened as he told me the story. A few years later he left
his big corporation job but he never did go back to
school to get a history degree. Half of him at least got
liberated. How he made peace with the rest of him is
impossible to know. Or maybe that is yet to come.

What happens if we should begin again and do not?
One thing is sure: the risks of not pursuing our deepest
gifts, our strongest passions, our need for higher purpose in life also are serious, not only for ourselves but
for those around us as well, whose happiness quotient
will be affected by our own. Frustration with what is,
the ennui that develops in the face of what has never
been, and the sense of emptiness that comes with leaving behind the part of ourselves that could have been
pursued but was not, are serious breaches of life.

Obviously there is a public risk in allowing ourselves to grow slowly, steadily into the resolution of
the self, but there is even worse risk if we attempt to
ignore it. Frustration triggered more by what is missing
in life than by what we are dealing with there saps our
energy for anything else. We get irritable with others.
We get even more disgusted with the self in us that we
have learned to dislike. Inertia fills the space where
love of life used to be. Emptiness colors and smothers
everything else we attempt to do.

Clearly, "It's too late for that now" is too great a burden to bear. When is it too late to start over? Never.
Not as long as we are alive and seeking even more out

of life. Grandma Moses knew that and began to paint in her late seventies; Beethoven, deaf as stone, knew that and went on composing long after he could hear what he wrote; Ronald Reagan knew that and left a career in film for a career in politics at the age of fifty-five and for the presidency at sixty-nine.

Life is lived in stages. Everything in one stage is simply a prelude to the next, where the lessons will be even more life-giving than before and past learnings will take on new value.

"We are always beginning to live," the Roman poet Manilius wrote in the first century, "but are never living." We are always becoming, never at any given moment totally and finally complete. The only answer, then, to the question of whether we should start over again is to do what we must in every stage and be ready, when the time comes, to go on living fully in the next one.

The important thing is not to stop questioning.

EINSTEIN

22.

WHERE IS GOD IN ALL OF THIS?

*"How do I know that what I'm doing
is God's will for me and not just my own
interests at work?"*

*"Where do you suppose those interests
came from anyway?"*

As a young monastic, I heard a story that suspended life for me in midair. "What do you do in a monastery?" the disciples asked the elder. And the elder answered, "Oh, we fall and we get up and we fall and we get up and we fall and we get up again." Nothing and no one, I could see, could possibly be perfect. Life was a process, not an event, not a competition, not a game of winner take all. On the contrary. "Life," Schopenhauer wrote, "is a language in which certain truths are conveyed to us; if we could learn them in some other way, we should not live."

At that moment I began to understand not only what life is about but who God is, as well. Life, I learned, is about seeking God here, and then, as the years go by—as we fall and get up, fail and fail again in the process of learning how to live—become gradually more and more fused, steeped, dissolved into that image of God ourselves.

But even that learning is slow in coming. Instead, the specter of perfectionism has long been the scourge of every religion. It challenges the notion of everything else we say about the goodness of God, the mercy of God, the love of God. In lieu of love, perfectionism teaches us fear of a remote God who knows our nature and ignores it. It engraves on our minds the image of a God who lies in wait to test our fidelity by trapping us in our imperfections. It dims for us the vision of the God who created us precisely so we could grow gently and gradually into the fullness of ourselves, so we could ourselves become as close to the image of the creator God on earth as humanly possible.

As a result, we call ourselves religious—meaning lovers of God—but then go through life assuming the very worst about who and what this God is. We look over our shoulders constantly to see if we're being good enough, right enough, perfect enough to merit a return to the source of our existence. We come to doubt not only the love of a loving God but we learn to doubt ourselves, as well.

All religions have a specific concept for it but, at the end of the day, it all means the same thing. Nirvana, enlightenment, union with God, heaven—whatever language any tradition uses to describe the readiness of the soul for reabsorption in divine reality—always depends, in the end, on finally doing things right.

Karma or reincarnation or purification or sinlessness—the perfect adherence to the rules of the faith as they have been defined through the ages—measures our trek through time. When we have finally passed every test and eliminated every speck of human degradation from our psyches, we're told, we will be ready to be consumed into the presence of God, we will be without sin, we will have become perfect.

The one problem, of course, is that if the God who made us is perfect, then that God knows that we are not. Because that God did not make us so. And if we are human, imperfect by nature, then perfection is fundamentally impossible for us. We can be perfectly loving and perfectly willing and perfectly committed to the will of God but we will not be perfectly perfect all the time. We will all "fall and get up, fall and get up, fall and get up" time after time after time.

We will find our way through life one fall at a time, one stone wall at a time, one blind spot at a time, one misunderstanding at a time, one fear at a time. One more bit of arrogance toppled, one more bit of self-doubt confirmed, at a time.

Which means that determining what we are meant to do with our lives will necessarily unfold slowly and tentatively. Just as we grow slowly and tentatively, so will our understanding and awareness of what we are meant to do in life develop the same way.

At the age of five we want to be firefighters, police officers, truck drivers, doctors ballerinas, teachers, and pilots. Then two years later, more experienced, more thoughtful, and more self aware, we mention none of those things. As adults, we aren't that much different from our younger selves. We go from one direction to another for years, trying this, researching that, discovering barriers and boundaries, excitements and joys that give us pause, or, perhaps, that completely redirect us. The only difference is that we are usually far less open about our ambivalence, our arrogance, our fears of trying things now than we were when we were children.

We are also more aware now of what it may cost us to become the full range of ourselves: We know the price now of leaving home, of struggling to support ourselves, of the confusion that comes with dealing with uncertainties. We know the value now of facing up to our failures, of discovering what success is really about, of learning to go the road alone. We have come now to appreciate the worth of admitting our limitations. We have come to realize the freedom that comes with becoming who we are rather than allowing ourselves to become a poor copy of someone else.

But there are three clues and three cautions about

what it means to discern what we are meant to do in life if we really want to do the will of God.

The clues are clear: the will of God for us is that we fulfill what we have been given, what we were born with, what we are in the raw.

First, to do what we are meant to do in life we must have whatever natural potential it takes to do it. And more than that, we must be willing to pay the price to succeed at it. Perhaps the saddest, most damning words in the lexicon of life are "She never lived up to her potential." Nothing comes from nothing attempted. The greatest geniuses practice before they play in public.

Second, to do what we are meant to do in life, we must have great passion for it. What we do with our life is our gift to the human race. To do it well, we must give it everything we have so that the work of God on earth can be done through us. The effort we fail to give to what must be done will only delay its coming to life. To say that we are committed to doing peace work but do it poorly or seldom or carelessly or irresponsibly only means that many will go on suffering even longer from the effects of violence.

Third, to do what we are really meant to do in life, we must see what we are doing not only as the real purpose of our life but also the ultimate legacy of our life. It is what we will leave behind us for future generations to build on. God did not finish creation; God started it. Its ongoing development God leaves to us.

What we do in life makes us the hands of God in living flesh and blood.

Finally, there are three cautions to be considered as we go stolidly on from day to day, trying to discover such raw potential in us, such deep passion, such holy purpose.

First, however long it takes to feel all the pieces go together inside of us, we must remain committed to the pursuit of our own wholeness. I passed a television set recently just in time to hear a young middle-aged woman being interviewed about her work with people who suffer from chronic depression. "What made you do this?" the reporter asked. And the woman answered, "I got into it by accident," she said. "I responded to a situation and discovered that I was good at it. Now all I can say is that I know that this is what I'm meant to do in life."

The point at which we hear the voice inside of us say, "I know that I am meant to do this in life," is the point at which we become fully developed human beings. It is for that reason we are where we are. The pilgrimage to the self stops there.

Second, we must trust that we are being led in that direction. It is simply a matter of doing what our natural gifts and our greater world demand of us. At the end of that search is the true self, the holy self, the completed self.

Third, we must have patience for the journey. The society around us has created arbitrary checkpoints which in turn create arbitrary definitions of our own self-fulfillment. At twenty-one we are supposed to take on adulthood in all its dimensions. Except that all of those dimensions can't possibly be grasped yet. Experience counts; passion counts; opportunity counts.

At sixty-five we are supposed to be finished with what we were meant to be in life. Except that there is another third of life left to live yet at that age and a great deal more for our older, wiser selves to do.

Finally, a career is at best a part of life, not all of life. A job and a life are not necessarily equivalent. Simply to have a job does not mean that we are really doing what we are meant to do in life. That is for us to figure out.

God is not a vending machine that prints fortunes or a global positioning system that tells us where to go. We have been created with everything in us that we need in order to determine what we are meant to do in life. That is where God wants us to be, that is what God wants us to be doing, that is the will of God for us.

The Hasidic Masters tell a story that says it all, perhaps:

> One day a Jewish disciple asked the Master, "What good work shall I do to be acceptable to God?"
>
> "How should I know?" the Master said. "Your Bible says that Abraham practiced hospitality and God was with him. Elias loved

to pray and God was with him. David ruled a kingdom and God was with him, too."

"Is there some way," the disciple went on, "I can find my allotted work?"

And the Master answered him. "Yes, search for the deepest inclination of your heart and follow it."

It is coming to the completion of our best selves, it is in following the magnet in our hearts, that we become our whole selves. Then we will have come to fullness of life, to the flowering of our best gifts, to being what we were meant to be, to finding the reason for which we were born. Then, having followed the deepest inclination of our hearts, we will have discovered what life is really all about. And that is surely the will of God for us.

Life is a pure flame, and we live by an invisible sun within us.

THOMAS BROWNE

About the Author

JOAN CHITTISTER is an articulate social analyst and influential religious leader. For over thirty years she has put her energy into advocating for the critical questions impacting the global community. Courageous, passionate, and charged with energy, she is a much sought after speaker, counselor, and clear voice across all religions.

A Benedictine Sister of Erie, Pennsylvania, Sister Joan is an international lecturer and award-winning author of over forty books. She is the founder and executive director of Benetvision—a resource and research center for contemporary spirituality located in Erie.

Currently she serves as cochair of the Global Peace Initiative of Women, a partner organization of the UN, facilitating a worldwide network of women peace builders.

Sister Joan has received numerous awards and recognition for her work for justice, peace, and equality, especially for women in the church and in society, including the *U.S. Catholic* magazine award for Furthering the Cause of Women in the Church and twelve honorary degrees from U.S. colleges and universities. Ten of her books have received recognition from the Catholic Press Association.

She was prioress of the Benedictine Sisters of Erie for twelve years, received her master's degree from the University of Notre Dame, and received her doctorate from Penn State University in Speech Communications Theory. Additionally, she was an invited fellow and research associate at St. Edmund's College, Cambridge University.